The Definitive Guide to Forecasting Using W.D.Gann's Square of Nine

By Patrick Mikula

Copyright © 2003 by Patrick Mikula All Rights Reserved
First Edition: First Printing

ISBN 0-9650518-6-2

Published by
Mikula Forecasting Company
www.MikulaForecasting.com
P.O. Box 152672
Austin TX 78715-2672
USA

Important Notice:
No claim is made that the trading methods or ideas in this book will result in profits and will not result in losses. The contents of this book are not guaranteed to produce profits. Commodity futures or stock trading is a risky business and may not be suitable for all recipients of this book. Although the financial correlations contained in this book have been reliable in the past there is no guarantee by the book's author or distributors that they will work in the future. Each trader is responsible for his/her own actions in the markets, if any. The contents of this book are not, and should not be considered as an offer to buy or sell any commodity or futures contract or stock. Purchase of this book constitutes your agreement to this disclaimer and exempts its author and distributors from any liability or litigation.

Copyright Notice:
No part of this book may be reproduced without written permission from the publisher. No part of this book may be reproduced, stored in a retrieval system, or transmitted in any form or by any means, photocopying, electronic, mechanical, or otherwise, without the prior written permission of the publisher.

Mikula's Forecasting Library

Mikula Forecasting Company
Presents
Mikula's Forecasting Library
Which Currently includes the two Books Listed Below.

The Definitive Guide to Forecasting Using W.D.Gann's Square of Nine
ISBN 0-9650518-6-2

The Best Trendline Methods of Alan Andrews and Five New Trendline Techniques
ISBN 0-9650518-3-8

Table of Contents

CHAPTER 1: Introduction

W.D.Gann's Square of Nine .... Page 1

Construction & Variations of the Square of Nine .... Page 3

Mathematical Principles of the Square of Nine .... Page 5

Odd Square Numbers .... Page 5

Even Square Numbers .... Page 6

Square Number Half Way Points .... Page 7

Square Number Quarter Points .... Page 8

Diagonal Cross and Cardinal Cross .... Page 11

Formula for Calculating The Amount of Cells in a Rotation .... Page 12

Other Math Principles For Square Numbers and The Square Of Nine .... Page 13

Column and Row Square of Nine .... Page 14

Formula for Moving Around The Square of Nine .... Page 15

Numbers on the Circle Around the Square of Nine .... Page 17

Angle Overlays .... Page 28

Shape Overlays .... Page 31

Two Ways to Align an Overlay On The Square of Nine .... Page 33

The Correct Way to Align an Overlay On a Cell .... Page 36

Angle Degree for Each Cell .... Page 38

Price Chart Basics .... Page 42

Defining Pivots .... Page 43

Defining Support and Resistance Lines .... Page 43

Defining a Congestion Area .... Page 43

CHAPTER 2: Forecasting Prices:
Using Cell Numbers

Example 1 - Weekly S&P500 .... Page 44

Example 2 - Daily Live Cattle .... Page 46

Example 3 - Daily Euro Currency .... Page 48

Example 4 - Daily DJIA .... Page 51

Chapter 2 Review .... Page 53

CHAPTER 3: Forecasting Prices:
Using Cell Numbers and Overlays

Example 1 - Daily Crude Oil .... Page 54

Example 2 - Daily Coffee .... Page 56

Example 3 - Daily Gateway 2000, GTW .... Page 60

Example 4 - Daily Japanese Yen .... Page 62

Chapter 3 Review .... Page 65

CHAPTER 4: Forecasting Dates:
Using Cell Numbers

Example 1 - Weekly S&P500 ....Page 66

Example 2 - Daily Altera, ALTR .... Page 70

Example 3 - Intraday 15 Minute Honeywell, HON ....Page 74

Monthly Square..Page 78

Yearly Square.. Page 79

Chapter 4 Review .... Page 80

CHAPTER 5: Forecasting Dates:
Using Overlays and Historical Pivot Dates

Example 1 - Daily Continuous May Soybean Contract .... Page 81

Example 2 - Weekly Wendy's, WEN .... Page 86

Example 3 - Daily American Express, AXP .... Page 90

Chapter 5 Review .... Page 94

CHAPTER 6: Forecasting Prices:
Using Progression

Example 1 - Daily Soybean Oil .... Page 95

Example 2 - Daily Merck, MRK ....Page 99

Selecting the Increment .... Page 103

Chapter 6 Formula ....Page 104

Chapter 6 Review .... Page 104

CHAPTER 7: Forecasting Prices:
Using Progression and Overlays

Example 1 - Daily Procter & Gamble, PG ....Page 105

Example 2 - 15 Minute Procter & Gamble, PG ....Page 109

Example 3 - Weekly Cendant, CD ....Page 113

Chapter 7 Review .... Page 117

CHAPTER 8: Forecasting Prices:
Using Regression

Example 1 - Daily Teradyne Inc. TER ....Page 118

Example 2 - Weekly S&P500 ....Page 122

Selecting the Decrement ....Page 125

Chapter 8 Formula ....Page 126

Chapter 8 Review .... Page 126

CHAPTER 9: Forecasting Prices: Using Regression and Overlays

Example 1 - Daily Wheat .... Page 127

Example 2 - Daily NASDAQ Index .... Page 132

Example 3 - Daily Corn .... Page 136

Chapter 9 Review .... Page 138

CHAPTER 10: Forecasting Prices: Using a Zero Base

Example 1 - Daily Minnesota Mining & Manufacturing Co., MMM .... Page 139

Example 2 - Daily Gold .... Page 142

Chapter 10 Formula .... Page 145

Chapter 10 Review .... Page 145

CHAPTER 11: Forecasting Prices: Using a Zero Base and Overlays

Example 1 - Daily Iomega Corp. IOM .... Page 146

Example 2 - Daily Wellpoint Health Network, WLP .... Page 149

Chapter 11 Formula .... Page 151

Chapter 11 Review .... Page 151

CHAPTER 12: Forecasting Dates: Using Shape Overlays

Example 1 - Daily Wheat .... Page 152

Example 2 - 5 Minute Minnesota Mining & Manufacturing Co., MMM .... Page 155

Example 3 - 5 Minute Disney, DIS .... Page 158

Chapter 12 Review .... Page 161

CHAPTER 13: Price and Time Forecasting Grid #1

How to Create and Use Price and Time Forecasting Grid #1 .... Page 162

Example 1 - Daily CRB Commodity Index .... Page 166

Example 2 - 15 Minute Amazon.com, AMZN .... Page 168

Chapter 13 Review .... Page 170

CHAPTER 14: Price and Time Forecasting Grid #2

How to Create and Use Price and Time Forecasting Grid #2 .... Page 171

Example 1 - Weekly S&P500 Index .... Page 174

Example 2 - 15 Minute Symantec Corp., SYMC .... Page 177

Chapter 14 Review .... Page 179

CHAPTER 15: Mikula's Square of Nine Planetary Angles

How to Draw Mikula's Square of Nine Planetary Angles .... Page 180

Example 1 - Daily NASDAQ Stock Index .... Page 185

Example 2 - Daily Euro-Currency .... Page 186

Example 3 - Daily Soybeans .... Page 188

Chapter 15 Review .... Page 189

CHAPTER 16: Mikula's Square of Nine High-Low Forecast Indicator

Required User Inputs .... Page 190

Formula and Calculation Procedure .... Page 190

Sample Calculation .... Page 191

Example 1 - Daily NASDAQ Index .... Page 193

Example 2 - Daily Soybeans .... Page 194

Chapter 16 Review .... Page 195

CHAPTER 17: Mikula's Square of Nine Over Under Indicator

Required User Inputs .... Page 196

Formula and Calculation Procedure .... Page 196

Sample Calculation .... Page 198

Example 1 - Daily Corn .... Page 199

Example 2 - Daily Johnson & Johnson, JNJ .... Page 200

Example 3 - Daily Baker Hughs Inc., BHI .... Page 201

Chapter 17 Review .... Page 202

Appendix 1: Index of Commodity Values

Index of Commodity Values .... Page 203

CHAPTER 1: Introduction

W.D.Gann's Square of Nine

W.D.Gann was a financial advisor and trader in the stock and commodity markets during the first half of the 20th century. In the 1920s, W.D.Gann developed the Square of Nine as a financial tool for trading and forecasting. The methods for using the Square of Nine were taught by W.D.Gann in his private financial seminars and later in his written trading courses. This book shows every major technique for forecasting using the Square of Nine. In referring to the Square of Nine, W.D.Gann also used the names "Odd Square" and "Master Price and Time Calculator." This book uses only the name Square of Nine. Figure 1 on the next page shows a basic Square of Nine.

On Figure 1, there are two sets of numbers. One set is on the circle around the outside of the square. The second set of numbers is on the face of the square. W.D.Gann placed the outer circle's 0° mark at the center right and he counted the degrees counter clockwise. The numbers on the face of the square move clockwise. In this chapter, the numbers on the face of the square are explained first and then the degrees around the outside are explained.

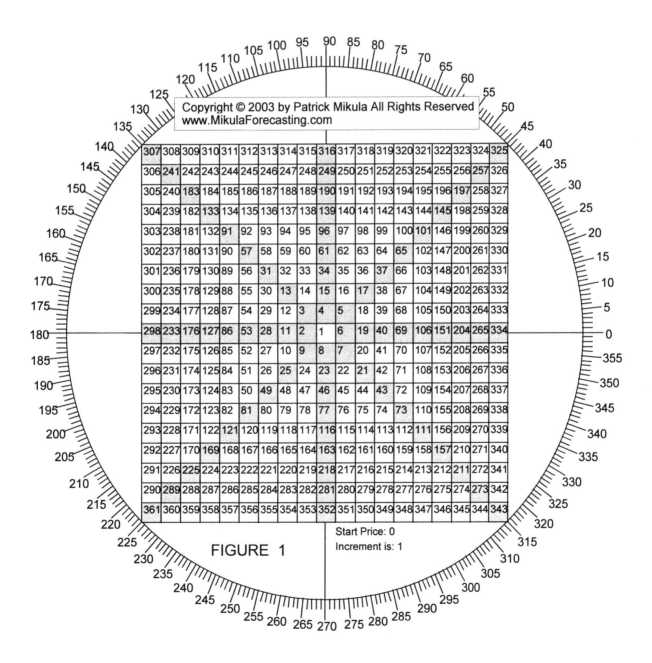

FIGURE 1

Start Price: 0
Increment is: 1

Construction & Variations of the Square of Nine

W.D.Gann used the words "square" and "cycle" when referring to a 360° movement of numbers on the Square of Nine. For example, on Figure 2, moving from 50 to 81 is one 360° movement. Gann called this movement a square or a cycle. However, these two words have double or triple meanings which make an advanced discussion of the Square of Nine confusing. Therefore, this book uses the word, "rotation" to refer to one 360° movement on the Square of Nine. On Figure 2, the background of each rotation alternates between white and gray. W.D.Gann identified a rotation by the largest number in that rotation. It is the number which always ends the rotation. For example, the rotation which runs from 82 to 121 is identified as the rotation ending on 121 or the rotation of 121.

W.D.Gann made his Square on Nine on graph paper and each number was placed in a graph square. We refer to a square that contains a single number as a cell. On the Square on Nine below, the number 147 is in cell 147.

Figure 2

133	134	135	136	137	138	139	140	141	142	143	144	145
132	91	92	93	94	95	96	97	98	99	100	101	146
131	90	57	58	59	60	61	62	63	64	65	102	147
130	89	56	31	32	33	34	35	36	37	66	103	148
129	88	55	30	13	14	15	16	17	38	67	104	149
128	87	54	29	12	3	4	5	18	39	68	105	150
127	86	53	28	11	2	1	6	19	40	69	106	151
126	85	52	27	10	9	8	7	20	41	70	107	152
125	84	51	26	25	24	23	22	21	42	71	108	153
124	83	50	49	48	47	46	45	44	43	72	109	154
123	82	81	80	79	78	77	76	75	74	73	110	155
122	121	120	119	118	117	116	115	114	113	112	111	156
169	168	167	166	165	164	163	162	161	160	159	158	157

This Rotation moves from 122 to 169

This Rotation moves from 82 to 121

On the examples of the Square of Nine shown so far, the numbers on the face of the square move in a clockwise rotation. A study of W.D.Gann's private work reveals that W.D.Gann made a few Square of Nine charts which rotated counter clockwise. On this page there are two simple Square of Nine illustrations. Figure 3 on the left, shows the numbers rotating clockwise. Figure 4 on the right, shows the numbers rotating counter clockwise. The majority of W.D.Gann's Square of Nine were made to rotate clockwise. I have studied the Square of Nine rotating in both directions and the results are the same. It does not matter which direction is used. This book uses only the clockwise rotation because this is the direction W.D.Gann used most frequently.

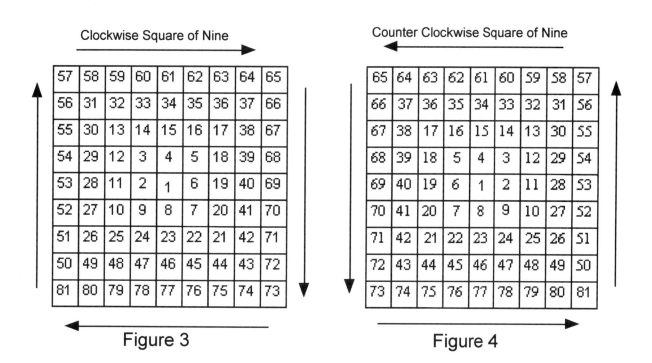

Figure 3   Figure 4

Mathematical Principles of the Square of Nine

Odd Square Numbers

On Figure 5, there is a circle around each odd square number. These numbers are 9, 25, 49, 81, 121 and so on. The number 9 is the square of 3, (3x3=9). The next numbers are the squares of 5, 7, 9, and 11. The squares of odd numbers are always aligned through the lower left corners of each rotation. The squares of odd numbers are the last number in each rotation. After the number 9, the Square of Nine moves outward and starts a new rotation which runs from 10 to 25. After 25, the Square of Nine moves to the next larger rotation and runs from 26 to 49. The Square of Nine gets its name from the fact that the first full rotation is complete on the number 9.

Figure 5

183	184	185	186	187	188	189	190	191	192	193	194	195	196	197
182	133	134	135	136	137	138	139	140	141	142	143	144	145	198
181	132	91	92	93	94	95	96	97	98	99	100	101	146	199
180	131	90	57	58	59	60	61	62	63	64	65	102	147	200
179	130	89	56	31	32	33	34	35	36	37	66	103	148	201
178	129	88	55	30	13	14	15	16	17	38	67	104	149	202
177	128	87	54	29	12	3	4	5	18	39	68	105	150	203
176	127	86	53	28	11	2	1	6	19	40	69	106	151	204
175	126	85	52	27	10	9	8	7	20	41	70	107	152	205
174	125	84	51	26	25	24	23	22	21	42	71	108	153	206
173	124	83	50	49	48	47	46	45	44	43	72	109	154	207
172	123	82	81	80	79	78	77	76	75	74	73	110	155	208
171	122	121	120	119	118	117	116	115	114	113	112	111	156	209
170	169	168	167	166	165	164	163	162	161	160	159	158	157	210
225	224	223	222	221	220	219	218	217	216	215	214	213	212	211

Even Square Numbers

Figure 6 shows a circle around each even square number. Starting on the number 4 and moving upward to the top right corner, all the even square numbers are aligned. These numbers are 4, 16, 36, 64, 100 and so on. The number 4 is the square of 2, (2x2=4). The next numbers are the squares of 4, 6, 8, 10, and continue on. A comparison of the positions of the odd square numbers shown on the previous page, and the even square numbers on this page, shows the odd and even square numbers are opposite each other on the Square of Nine.

Figure 6

183	184	185	186	187	188	189	190	191	192	193	194	195	196	197
182	133	134	135	136	137	138	139	140	141	142	143	144	145	198
181	132	91	92	93	94	95	96	97	98	99	100	101	146	199
180	131	90	57	58	59	60	61	62	63	64	65	102	147	200
179	130	89	56	31	32	33	34	35	36	37	66	103	148	201
178	129	88	55	30	13	14	15	16	17	38	67	104	149	202
177	128	87	54	29	12	3	4	5	18	39	68	105	150	203
176	127	86	53	28	11	2	1	6	19	40	69	106	151	204
175	126	85	52	27	10	9	8	7	20	41	70	107	152	205
174	125	84	51	26	25	24	23	22	21	42	71	108	153	206
173	124	83	50	49	48	47	46	45	44	43	72	109	154	207
172	123	82	81	80	79	78	77	76	75	74	73	110	155	208
171	122	121	120	119	118	117	116	115	114	113	112	111	156	209
170	169	168	167	166	165	164	163	162	161	160	159	158	157	210
225	224	223	222	221	220	219	218	217	216	215	214	213	212	211

Square Number Half Way Points

On the Square of Nine, the half way points between an even square number and the next higher odd square number are all aligned sloping downward to the lower right corner. For example, the half way point between 64 and 81 is 72.5. The half way point between 100 and 121 is 110.5; the half way point between 144 and 169 is 156.5. Figure 7 shows a line marking the approximate locations of these half way points as they slope downward and right.

The half way points between odd square numbers and the next higher even square number are all aligned sloping upward to the top left corner. The half way point between 81 and 100 is 90.5; the half way point between 121 and 144 is 132.5; the half way point between 169 and 196 is 182.5. Figure 7 has another line marking the approximate locations of these half way points. This line illustrates the pattern leading upward and left.

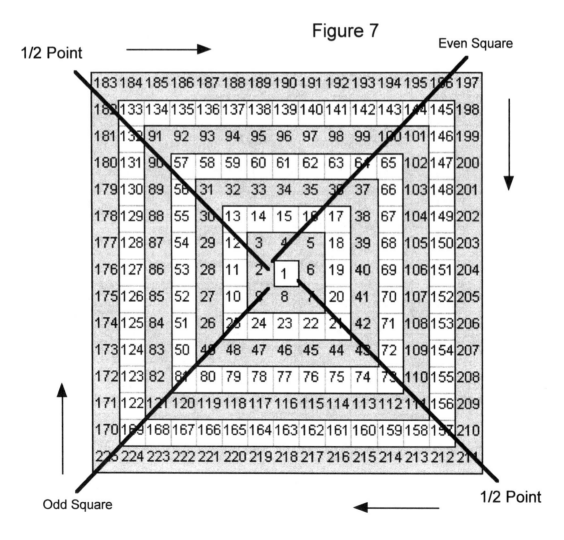

Figure 7

Square Number Quarter Points

As the numbers on the Square of Nine progress from even square numbers to odd square numbers, or from odd square numbers to even square numbers, the progression first encounters quarter points, then halfway points and finally third quarter points. The half way point locations are detailed on the previous page.

The first quarter points, are located on the right side horizontal axis and the left side horizontal axis. For example, on Figure 8, between the even square number, 196, and the next odd square number, 225, the first quarter point is 203.25.

The location of the third quarter points are on the lower vertical axis and the upper vertical axis. For example, on Figure 8, the third quarter point between odd square 169, and even square 196, is 189.25.

The first quarter points and third quarter points are not whole numbers. Numbers such as 203.25 are not listed on the Square of Nine. These numbers are between the whole numbers that are on the Square of Nine.

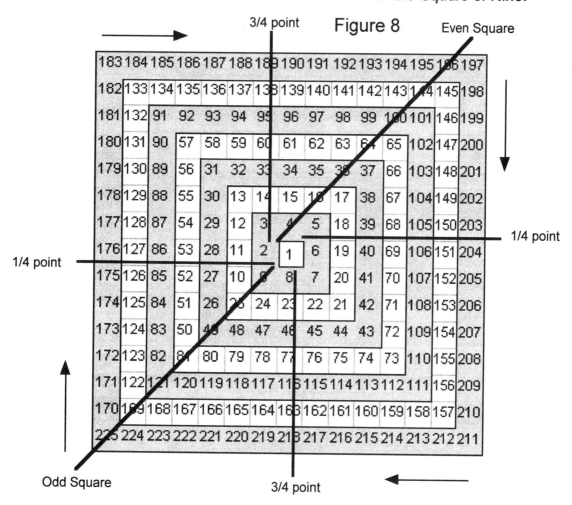

Figure 8

The Square of Nine in Figure 9 shows the location of the quarter points and half way points between the odd and even square numbers.

1/4: One Quarter Points	
Even square # to odd square #	Right horizontal axis
Odd square # to even square #	Left horizontal axis
1/2: Half Way Points	
Even square # to odd square #	Downward and right axis
Odd square # to even square #	Upward and left axis
3/4: Three Quarter Points	
Even square # to odd Square #	Lower vertical axis
Odd Square # to even square #	Upper vertical axis

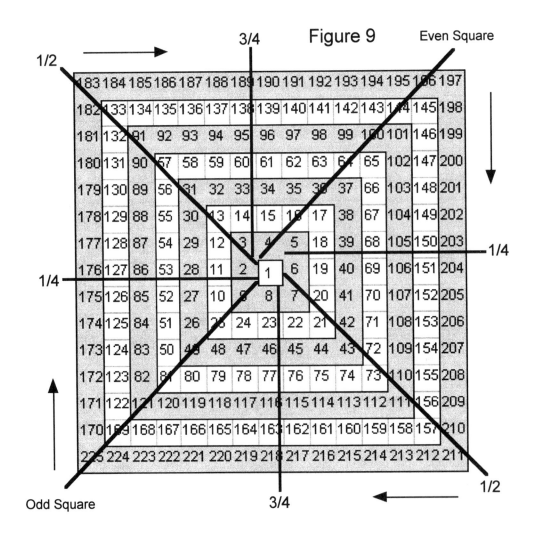

Figure 9

The Square of Nine in Figure 10 shows the same points seen as in Figure 9. These points are now used to divide one full rotation from odd square to the next odd square. In this situation, these points represent the one-eight increments around one full rotation.

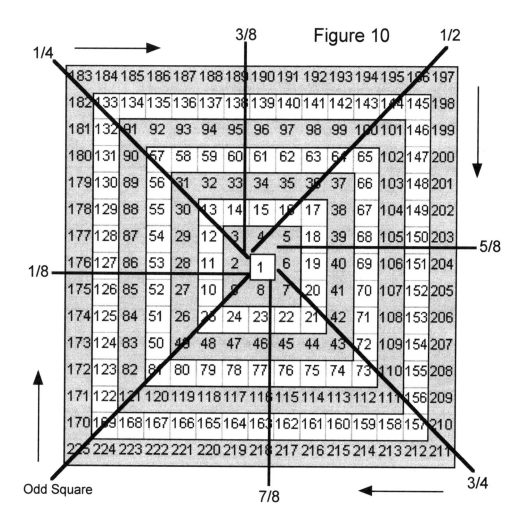

Figure 10

Diagonal Cross and Cardinal Cross

The simplest rule W.D.Gann provided for using the Square of Nine is that the cells which fall on the diagonal cross and cardinal cross are important for market analysis. The diagonal cross looks like the letter X and the cardinal cross looks like the plus symbol, +. Figure 11 shows a Square of Nine with both the diagonal cross and cardinal cross highlighted.

W.D.Gann placed importance on the diagonal cross because the angles mark the approximate locations of the odd square numbers, even square numbers and the half way points between the odd and even square numbers.

W.D.Gann placed importance on the cardinal cross because the angles mark the approximate location of the quarter points between the odd and even square numbers on the Square of Nine.

Figure 11

183	184	185	186	187	188	189	190	191	192	193	194	195	196	197
182	133	134	135	136	137	138	139	140	141	142	143	144	145	198
181	132	91	92	93	94	95	96	97	98	99	100	101	146	199
180	131	90	57	58	59	60	61	62	63	64	65	102	147	200
179	130	89	56	31	32	33	34	35	36	37	66	103	148	201
178	129	88	55	30	13	14	15	16	17	38	67	104	149	202
177	128	87	54	29	12	3	4	5	18	39	68	105	150	203
176	127	86	53	28	11	2	1	6	19	40	69	106	151	204
175	126	85	52	27	10	9	8	7	20	41	70	107	152	205
174	125	84	51	26	25	24	23	22	21	42	71	108	153	206
173	124	83	50	49	48	47	46	45	44	43	72	109	154	207
172	123	82	81	80	79	78	77	76	75	74	73	110	155	208
171	122	121	120	119	118	117	116	115	114	113	112	111	156	209
170	169	168	167	166	165	164	163	162	161	160	159	158	157	210
225	224	223	222	221	220	219	218	217	216	215	214	213	212	211

Formula for Calculating the Amount of Cells in a Rotation

The Square of Nine layout is not based solely on the position of the odd and even square numbers. Calculations on the Square of Nine are also based on the number eight (8). Each rotation on the Square of Nine contains eight more numbers than the previous rotation. The first rotation runs from 2 to 9 and has eight numbers. The second rotation has 16 numbers, 8+8=16. The third rotation has 24 numbers, 16+8=24. This is shown below for the first nine rotations on the Square of Nine.

Rotation 1 has 8 numbers from 2 to 9
Rotation 2 has 16 numbers (8+8=16) from   10 to 25
Rotation 3 has 24 numbers (16+8=24) from   26 to 49
Rotation 4 has 32 numbers (24+8=32) from   50 to 81
Rotation 5 has 40 numbers (32+8=40) from   82 to 121
Rotation 6 has 48 numbers (40+8=48) from 122 to 169
Rotation 7 has 56 numbers (48+8=56) from 170 to 225
Rotation 8 has 64 numbers (56+8=64) from 226 to 289
Rotation 9 has 72 numbers (64+8=72) from 290 to 361

Steps to calculate the number of cells in a Square of Nine rotation
Step 1.) Start with the odd square number which ends the rotation (Example: 361)
Step 2.) Find the square root of the number from step 1. (Example: 361 SR = 19)
Step 3.) Divide by 2 the answer from step 2 (Example: 19/2 = 9.5)
Step 4.) Subtract 0.5 from the answer in step 3 (Example: 9.5 - 0.5 = 9)
Step 5.) Multiply the step 4 answer times 8 (Example 9 x 8 = 72)
There are 72 cells in the rotation which ends on 361.

Other Math Principles For Square Numbers and the Square of Nine

Each rotation on the Square of Nine ends on an odd square number. All odd square numbers minus one, divide evenly by 8. For example, 13 x 13 = 169 and 169 - 1 = 168 and 168 / 8 = 21. Again, 97 x 97 = 9409 and 9409 - 1 = 9408 and 9408 / 8 = 1176.

Here is an interesting fact about even square numbers. The number four divides all even number squares exactly. For example, 16 is an even number and 16 x 16 = 256 and 256 / 4 = 64. When an even number square is divided by four, the resulting number is always another even square number. To say this another way, one fourth of an even number square is always an even square number. For example, 12 x 12 = 144 and 144 / 4 = 36 and 36 is the square of 6. Another example of this is 360 x 360 = 129600 and 129600 / 4 = 32400 and 32400 is the square of 180.

To calculate the number of cells across the bottom of a Square of Nine, simply take the square root of the odd square which ends the Square of Nine. For example, on the Square of Nine in Figure 11, the last number on the square is 225. The square root of 225 is 15 and 15 is the number of cells across the bottom of the Square of Nine from 211 to 225.

Steps to calculate the number of cells across the bottom of a Square of Nine

Step 1.) Start with the odd square number which ends the square (Example: 225)
Step 2.) Find the square root of the number from step 1. (Example: 225 SR = 15)
There are 15 cells across the bottom of the Square of Nine ending on 225

Column and Row Square of Nine

Two additional ways to look at the rotations of the Square of Nine are in column and row form. Seen below are the first four rotations of the Square of Nine in column form and in row form. It is easy to see that each column is larger than the previous column by the same amount. Each column adds eight numbers. The rows show the same thing; each row is longer than the previous row by eight numbers.

```
                        81
                        80
                        79
                        78
                        77
                        76
                        75
                        74
                   49   73
                   48   72
                   47   71
                   46   70
                   45   69
                   44   68
                   43   67
                   42   66
              25   41   65
              24   40   64
              23   39   63
              22   38   62
              21   37   61
              20   36   60
              19   35   59
              18   34   58
         9    17   33   57
         8    16   32   56
         7    15   31   55
         6    14   30   54
         5    13   29   53
         4    12   28   52
         3    11   27   51
    1    2    10   26   50
```

Here are the first four rotations of the Square of Nine laid out in rows.

1
2 3 4 5 6 7 8 9
10 11 12 13 14 15 16 17 18 19 20 21 22 23 24 25
26 27 28 29 30 31 32 33 34 35 36 37 38 39 40 41 42 43 44 45 46 47 48 49
50 51 52 53 54 55 56 57 58 59 60 61 62 63 64 65 66 67 68 69 70 71 72 73 74 75 76 77 78 79 80 81

Formula for Moving Around the Square of Nine

There is an important formula for moving around the face of the Square of Nine. This formula is used to calculate two technical indicators in Chapter 16 and 17. From a starting number on the face of the Square of Nine, it is possible to follow the number progression back to the same location but one rotation inward to the center or one rotation outward. For example, starting on the number 225 and moving inward, one rotation arrives at 169. To move from 225 to 169 mathematically, start with 225. Take the square root $\sqrt{}$ of 225 which is 15. Subtract 2 from 15 which is 13. Finally, square 13 which is 169.

On the Square of Nine, each rotation has more numbers than the previous rotation. Due to this fact, most of the movements around the face of the Square of Nine do not result in a whole number. For example, the Square of Nine in Figure 11 shows the number 211 in the lower right corner. It looks like a move of one rotation inward to the center reaches 157. This is not the case. The calculation produces the number 156.89664. Only if you start on an odd square number such as 81, 121, 169 or 225 and move in increments of one-half rotation, are the results a whole number.

Steps to move around on the face of the Square of Nine is as follows.

Step 1.) Select a starting number from the face of the Square of Nine.
Step 2.) Calculate the square root of the starting number.
Step 3.) Decide the distance to move inward or outward.
    a.) To reduce the starting number by one rotation subtract 2
    b.) To reduce the starting number by one-half rotation subtract 1
    c.) To reduce the starting number by one-fourth rotation subtract 0.5
    d.) To reduce the starting number by one-eight rotation subtract 0.25

    e.) To increase the starting number by one rotation add 2
    f.) To increase the starting number by one-half rotation add 1
    g.) To increase the starting number by one-fourth rotation add 0.5
    h.) To increase the starting number by one-eight rotation add 0.25

Step 4.) Finally, square the new number.

The examples below can be used to develop a solid understanding of this formula.

Example 1: Start on 78 and move outward one-half rotation
Square Root $\sqrt{}$ 78 = 8.8317608
Add 1 = 9.8317608
Square the new number = 96.66352

Example 2: Start on 130 and move inward one-eight rotation
Square Root √ 130 = 11.401754
Subtract 0.25 = 11.151754
Square the new number = 124.36161

Example 3: Start on 201 and move inward three rotations
Square Root √ 201 = 14.177446
Subtract 6 = 8.177446
Square the new number = 66.870623

Example 4: Start on 74 and move outward one and one-eighth rotation
Square Root √ 74 = 8.6023252
add 2.25 = 10.852325
Square the new number = 117.77295

When moving by a particular number of rotations from a starting number, calculate the value to add or subtract based on a full rotation equaling 2. Here are two more examples that deal with custom amounts of movement.

To move a starting number three- fourths of one rotation, calculate the number to add or subtract by multiplying 3/4 or 0.75 by 2. This yields 1.5.

Example 5: Start on 122 and move outward three- fourths of one rotation
Square Root √ 122 = 11.045361
add 1.5 = 12.545361
Square the new number = 157.38608

To move one and three-quarters rotations, which is 1.75 rotations, calculate the number to add or subtract by multiplying 1.75 by 2. This yields 3.5 (1.75 * 2).

Example 6: Start on 193 and move inward one and three-quarters rotations
Square Root √ 193 = 13.892443
Subtract 3.5 = 10.392443
Square the new number = 108.0028

Numbers on the Circle Around the Square of Nine

On the outer circle around the Square of Nine, the degree marks are added. W.D.Gann placed the 0° - 360° mark on the center right side. In addition to the degree marks, W.D.Gann added the dates of the year and the 24 hours of the day.

The Spring Equinox on March 21 is aligned on 0° - 360°. The Summer Solstice on June 21 is assigned to 90°. The Autumnal Equinox on September 22 is positioned on 180° and the Winter Solstice on December 21 is placed on 270°. This means the dates are not evenly divided around the square. From the Spring Equinox to the Summer Solstice there are 92 days. From the Summer Solstice to the Autumnal Equinox there are 93 days. From the Autumnal Equinox to the Winter Solstice there are 90 days. From the Winter Solstice back to the Spring Equinox there are 90 days except in a leap year. This equals 365 days, (92+93+90+90).

When W.D.Gann used the 24 hours of a day, he assigned 6:00 a.m. to the 0° - 360° mark. The earth rotates 1° every four minutes so the 24 hours are divided evenly into 360 four minute increments around the circle. The list below shows all 360° and the corresponding date and time. The signs of the zodiac and the compass directions are also added to the list.

Degree	Date	Time	Event	Direction	Zodiac
0°	March 21,	6:00 a.m.,	Spring Equinox,	East,	Aries ♈
1°	March 22,	6:04 a.m.			
2°	March 23,	6:08 a.m.			
3°	March 24,	6:12 a.m.			
4°	March 25,	6:16 a.m.			
5°	March 26,	6:20 a.m.			
6°	March 27,	6:24 a.m.			
7°	March 28,	6:28 a.m.			
8°	March 29,	6:32 a.m.			
9°	March 30,	6:36 a.m.			
10°	March 31,	6:40 a.m.			
11°	April 1,	6:44 a.m.			
12°	April 2,	6:48 a.m.			
13°	April 3,	6:52 a.m.			
14°	April 4,	6:56 a.m.			
15°	April 5,	7:00 a.m.			
16°	April 6,	7:04 a.m.			
17°	April 7,	7:08 a.m.			
18°	April 8,	7:12 a.m.			
19°	April 9,	7:16 a.m.			
20°	April 10,	7:20 a.m.			
21°	April 11,	7:24 a.m.			

Degree	Date	Time	
22°	April 12,	7:28 a.m.	
22.5°	April 13,	7:30 a.m.	
23°	April 14,	7:32 a.m.	
24°	April 15,	7:36 a.m.	
25°	April 16,	7:40 a.m.	
26°	April 17,	7:44 a.m.	
27°	April 18,	7:48 a.m.	
28°	April 19,	7:52 a.m.	
29°	April 20,	7:56 a.m.	
30°	April 21,	8:00 a.m.,	Taurus ♉
31°	April 22,	8:04 a.m.	
32°	April 23,	8:08 a.m.	
33°	April 24,	8:12 a.m.	
34°	April 25,	8:16 a.m.	
35°	April 26,	8:20 a.m.	
36°	April 27,	8:24 a.m.	
37°	April 28,	8:28 a.m.	
38°	April 29,	8:32 a.m.	
39°	April 30,	8:36 a.m.	
40°	May 1,	8:40 a.m.	
41°	May 2,	8:44 a.m.	
42°	May 3,	8:48 a.m.	
43°	May 4,	8:52 a.m.	
44°	May 5,	8:56 a.m.	
45°	May 6,	9:00 a.m.,	North East
46°	May 7,	9:04 a.m.	
47°	May 8,	9:08 a.m.	
48°	May 9,	9:12 a.m.	
49°	May 10,	9:16 a.m.	
50°	May 11,	9:20 a.m.	
51°	May 12,	9:24 a.m.	
52°	May 13,	9:28 a.m.	
53°	May 14,	9:32 a.m.	
54°	May 15,	9:36 a.m.	
55°	May 16,	9:40 a.m.	
56°	May 17,	9:44 a.m.	
57°	May 18,	9:48 a.m.	
58°	May 19,	9:52 a.m.	
59°	May 20,	9:56 a.m.	
60°	May 21,	10:00 a.m.,	Gemini ♊
61°	May 22,	10:04 a.m.	
62°	May 23,	10:08 a.m.	
63°	May 24,	10:12 a.m.	

Degree	Date	Time			
64°	May 25,	10:16 a.m.			
65°	May 26,	10:20 a.m.			
66°	May 27,	10:24 a.m.			
67°	May 28,	10:28 a.m.			
67.5°	May 29,	10:30 a.m.			
68°	May 30,	10:32 a.m.			
69°	May 31,	10:36 a.m.			
70°	June 1,	10:40 a.m.			
71°	June 2,	10:44 a.m.			
72°	June 3,	10:48 a.m.			
73°	June 4,	10:52 a.m.			
74°	June 5,	10:56 a.m.			
75°	June 6,	11:00 a.m.			
76°	June 7,	11:04 a.m.			
77°	June 8,	11:08 a.m.			
78°	June 9,	11:12 a.m.			
79°	June 10,	11:16 a.m.			
80°	June 11,	11:20 a.m.			
81°	June 12,	11:24 a.m.			
82°	June 13,	11:28 a.m.			
83°	June 14,	11:32 a.m.			
84°	June 15,	11:36 a.m.			
85°	June 16,	11:40 a.m.			
86°	June 17,	11:44 a.m.			
87°	June 18,	11:48 a.m.			
88°	June 19,	11:52 a.m.			
89°	June 20,	11:56 a.m.			
90°	June 21,	12:00 Noon,	Summer Solstice,	North,	Cancer ♋
91°	June 22,	12:04 p.m.			
92°	June 23,	12:08 p.m.			
93°	June 24,	12:12 p.m.			
94°	June 25,	12:16 p.m.			
95°	June 26,	12:20 p.m.			
96°	June 27,	12:24 p.m.			
97°	June 28,	12:28 p.m.			
98°	June 29,	12:32 p.m.			
99°	June 30,	12:36 p.m.			
100°	July 1,	12:40 p.m.			
101°	July 2,	12:44 p.m.			
101.5°	July 3,	12:46 p.m.			
102°	July 4,	12:48 p.m.			
103°	July 5,	12:52 p.m.			
104°	July 6,	12:56 p.m.			

105°	July 7,	1:00 p.m.	
106°	July 8,	1:04 p.m.	
107°	July 9,	1:08 p.m.	
108°	July 10,	1:12 p.m.	
109°	July 11,	1:16 p.m.	
110°	July 12,	1:20 p.m.	
111°	July 13,	1:24 p.m.	
112°	July 14,	1:28 p.m.	
112.5°	July 15,	1:30 p.m.	
113°	July 16,	1:32 p.m.	
114°	July 17,	1:36 p.m.	
115°	July 18,	1:40 p.m.	
116°	July 19,	1:44 p.m.	
117°	July 20,	1:48 p.m.	
118°	July 21,	1:52 p.m.	
119°	July 22,	1:56 p.m.	
120°	July 23,	2:00 p.m.,	Leo ♌
121°	July 24,	2:04 p.m.	
122°	July 25,	2:08 p.m.	
123°	July 26,	2:12 p.m.	
124°	July 27,	2:16 p.m.	
125°	July 28,	2:20 p.m.	
126°	July 29,	2:24 p.m.	
127°	July 30,	2:28 p.m.	
128°	July 31,	2:32 p.m.	
129°	August 1,	2:36 p.m.	
130°	August 2,	2:40 p.m.	
131°	August 3,	2:44 p.m.	
132°	August 4,	2:48 p.m.	
133°	August 5,	2:52 p.m.	
134°	August 6,	2:56 p.m.	
135°	August 7,	3:00 p.m.,	North West
136°	August 8,	3:04 p.m.	
137°	August 9,	3:08 p.m.	
138°	August 10,	3:12 p.m.	
139°	August 11,	3:16 p.m.	
140°	August 12,	3:20 p.m.	
141°	August 13,	3:24 p.m.	
142°	August 14,	3:28 p.m.	
143°	August 15,	3:32 p.m.	
144°	August 16,	3:36 p.m.	
145°	August 17,	3:40 p.m.	
146°	August 18,	3:44 p.m.	

147°	August 19,	3:48 p.m.		
148°	August 20,	3:52 p.m.		
149°	August 21,	3:56 p.m.		
150°	August 22,	4:00 p.m.,	Virgo ♍	
151°	August 23,	4:04 p.m.		
152°	August 24,	4:08 p.m.		
153°	August 25,	4:12 p.m.		
154°	August 26,	4:16 p.m.		
155°	August 27,	4:20 p.m.		
156°	August 28,	4:24 p.m.		
157°	August 29,	4:28 p.m.		
157.5°	August 30,	4:30 p.m.		
158°	August 31,	4:32 p.m.		
159°	September 1,	4:36 p.m.		
160°	September 2,	4:40 p.m.		
161°	September 3,	4:44 p.m.		
162°	September 4,	4:48 p.m.		
163°	September 5,	4:52 p.m.		
164°	September 6,	4:56 p.m.		
165°	September 7,	5:00 p.m.		
166°	September 8,	5:04 p.m.		
167°	September 9,	5:08 p.m.		
168°	September 10,	5:12 p.m.		
169°	September 11,	5:16 p.m.		
170°	September 12,	5:20 p.m.		
171°	September 13,	5:24 p.m.		
172°	September 14,	5:28 p.m.		
173°	September 15,	5:32 p.m.		
174°	September 16,	5:36 p.m.		
175°	September 17,	5:40 p.m.		
176°	September 18,	5:44 p.m.		
177°	September 19,	5:48 p.m.		
178°	September 20,	5:52 p.m.		
179°	September 21,	5:56 p.m.		
180°	September 22,	6:00 p.m.,	Autumnal Equinox, West,	Libra ♎
181°	September 23,	6:04 p.m.		
182°	September 24,	6:08 p.m.		
183°	September 25,	6:12 p.m.		
184°	September 26,	6:16 p.m.		
185°	September 27,	6:20 p.m.		
186°	September 28,	6:24 p.m.		
187°	September 29,	6:28 p.m.		
188°	September 30,	6:32 p.m.		

189°	October 1,	6:36 p.m.	
190°	October 2,	6:40 p.m.	
191°	October 3,	6:44 p.m.	
192°	October 4,	6:48 p.m.	
193°	October 5,	6:52 p.m.	
194°	October 6,	6:56 p.m.	
195°	October 7,	7:00 p.m.	
196°	October 8,	7:04 p.m.	
197°	October 9,	7:08 p.m.	
198°	October 10,	7:12 p.m.	
199°	October 11,	7:16 p.m.	
200°	October 12,	7:20 p.m.	
201°	October 13,	7:24 p.m.	
202°	October 14,	7:28 p.m.	
203°	October 15,	7:32 p.m.	
204°	October 16,	7:36 p.m.	
205°	October 17,	7:40 p.m.	
206°	October 18,	7:44 p.m.	
207°	October 19,	7:48 p.m.	
208°	October 20,	7:52 p.m.	
209°	October 21,	7:56 p.m.	
210°	October 22,	8:00 p.m.,	Scorpio ♏
211°	October 23,	8:04 p.m.	
212°	October 24,	8:08 p.m.	
213°	October 25,	8:12 p.m.	
214°	October 26,	8:16 p.m.	
215°	October 27,	8:20 p.m.	
216°	October 28,	8:24 p.m.	
217°	October 29,	8:28 p.m.	
218°	October 30,	8:32 p.m.	
219°	October 31,	8:36 p.m.	
220°	November 1,	8:40 p.m.	
221°	November 2,	8:44 p.m.	
222°	November 3,	8:48 p.m.	
223°	November 4,	8:52 p.m.	
224°	November 5,	8:56 p.m.	
225°	November 6,	9:00 p.m.,	South West
226°	November 7,	9:04 p.m.	
227°	November 8,	9:08 p.m.	
228°	November 9,	9:12 p.m.	
229°	November 10,	9:16 p.m.	
230°	November 11,	9:20 p.m.	
231°	November 12,	9:24 p.m.	

232°	November 13,	9:28 p.m.			
233°	November 14,	9:32 p.m.			
234°	November 15,	9:36 p.m.			
235°	November 16,	9:40 p.m.			
236°	November 17,	9:44 p.m.			
237°	November 18,	9:48 p.m.			
238°	November 19,	9:52 p.m.			
239°	November 20,	9:56 p.m.			
240°	November 21,	10:00 p.m.,	Sagittarius ♐		
241°	November 22,	10:04 p.m.			
242°	November 23,	10:08 p.m.			
243°	November 24,	10:12 p.m.			
244°	November 25,	10:16 p.m.			
245°	November 26,	10:20 p.m.			
246°	November 27,	10:24 p.m.			
247°	November 28,	10:28 p.m.			
248°	November 29,	10:32 p.m.			
249°	November 30,	10:36 p.m.			
250°	December 1,	10:40 p.m.			
251°	December 2,	10:44 p.m.			
252°	December 3,	10:48 p.m.			
253°	December 4,	10:52 p.m.			
254°	December 5,	10:56 p.m.			
255°	December 6,	11:00 p.m.			
256°	December 7,	11:04 p.m.			
257°	December 8,	11:08 p.m.			
258°	December 9,	11:12 p.m.			
259°	December 10,	11:16 p.m.			
260°	December 11,	11:20 p.m.			
261°	December 12,	11:24 p.m.			
262°	December 13,	11:28 p.m.			
263°	December 14,	11:32 p.m.			
264°	December 15,	11:36 p.m.			
265°	December 16,	11:40 p.m.			
266°	December 17,	11:44 p.m.			
267°	December 18,	11:48 p.m.			
268°	December 19,	11:52 p.m.			
269°	December 20,	11:56 p.m.			
270°	December 21,	12:00 midnight,	Winter Solstice,	South,	Capricorn ♑
271°	December 22,	12:04 a.m.			
272°	December 23,	12:08 a.m.			
273°	December 24,	12:12 a.m.			
274°	December 25,	12:16 a.m.			

Degree	Date	Time	
275°	December 26,	12:20 a.m.	
276°	December 27,	12:24 a.m.	
277°	December 28,	12:28 a.m.	
278°	December 29,	12:32 a.m.	
279°	December 30,	12:36 a.m.	
280°	December 31,	12:40 a.m.	
281°	January 1,	12:44 a.m.	
282°	January 2,	12:48 a.m.	
283°	January 3,	12:52 a.m.	
284°	January 4,	12:56 a.m.	
285°	January 5,	1:00 a.m.	
286°	January 6,	1:04 a.m.	
287°	January 7,	1:08 a.m.	
288°	January 8,	1:12 a.m.	
289°	January 9,	1:16 a.m.	
290°	January 10,	1:20 a.m.	
291°	January 11,	1:24 a.m.	
292°	January 12,	1:28 a.m.	
293°	January 13,	1:32 a.m.	
294°	January 14,	1:36 a.m.	
295°	January 15,	1:40 a.m.	
296°	January 16,	1:44 a.m.	
297°	January 17,	1:48 a.m.	
298°	January 18,	1:52 a.m.	
299°	January 19,	1:56 a.m.	
300°	January 20,	2:00 a.m.,	Aquarius ♒
301°	January 21,	2:04 a.m.	
302°	January 22,	2:08 a.m.	
303°	January 23,	2:12 a.m.	
304°	January 24,	2:16 a.m.	
305°	January 25,	2:20 a.m.	
306°	January 26,	2:24 a.m.	
307°	January 27,	2:28 a.m.	
308°	January 28,	2:32 a.m.	
309°	January 29,	2:36 a.m.	
310°	January 30,	2:40 a.m.	
311°	January 31,	2:44 a.m	
312°	February 1,	2:48 a.m.	
313°	February 2,	2:52 a.m.	
314°	February 2,	2:56 a.m.	
315°	February 4,	3:00 a.m.	
316°	February 5,	3:04 a.m.	
317°	February 6,	3:08 a.m.	

318°	February 7,	3:12 a.m.			
319°	February 8,	3:16 a.m.			
320°	February 9,	3:20 a.m.			
321°	February 10,	3:24 a.m.			
322°	February 11,	3:28 a.m.			
323°	February 12,	3:32 a.m.			
324°	February 13,	3:36 a.m.			
325°	February 14,	3:40 a.m.			
326°	February 15,	3:44 a.m.			
327°	February 16,	3:48 a.m.			
328°	February 17,	3:52 a.m.			
329°	February 18,	3:56 a.m.			
330°	February 19,	4:00 a.m.	Pisces ♓		
331°	February 20,	4:04 a.m.			
332°	February 21,	4:08 a.m.			
333°	February 22,	4:12 a.m.			
334°	February 23,	4:16 a.m.			
335°	February 24,	4:20 a.m.			
336°	February 25,	4:24 a.m.			
337°	February 26,	4:28 a.m.			
338°	February 27,	4:32 a.m.			
339°	February 28,	4:36 a.m.			
340°	March 1,	4:40 a.m.			
341°	March 2,	4:44 a.m.			
342°	March 3,	4:48 a.m.			
343°	March 4,	4:52 a.m.			
344°	March 5,	4:56 a.m.			
345°	March 6,	5:00 a.m.			
346°	March 7,	5:04 a.m.			
347°	March 8,	5:08 a.m.			
348°	March 9,	5:12 a.m.			
349°	March 10,	5:16 a.m.			
350°	March 11,	5:20 a.m.			
351°	March 12,	5:24 a.m.			
352°	March 13,	5:28 a.m.			
353°	March 14,	5:32 a.m.			
354°	March 15,	5:36 a.m.			
355°	March 16,	5:40 a.m.			
356°	March 17,	5:44 a.m.			
357°	March 18,	5:48 a.m.			
358°	March 19,	5:52 a.m.			
359°	March 20,	5:56 a.m.			
360°	March 21,	6:00 a.m.,	Spring Equinox,	East,	Aries ♈

When he used the Square of Nine, W.D.Gann drew lines from the center of the square to the outer circle that holds the degrees. These lines are used with several Square of Nine forecasting methods. W.D.Gann identified these lines as angles. They were designated by the degree they touched on the outer circle. For example, Figure 12 has a line drawn from the center of the square to the 70° mark on the outer circle. This line is identified as the 70° angle. There is another line drawn from the center to the 200° mark. This line is the 200° angle. This is not the traditional geometric definition of an angle but is how W.D.Gann identified these lines so we are using his terminology.

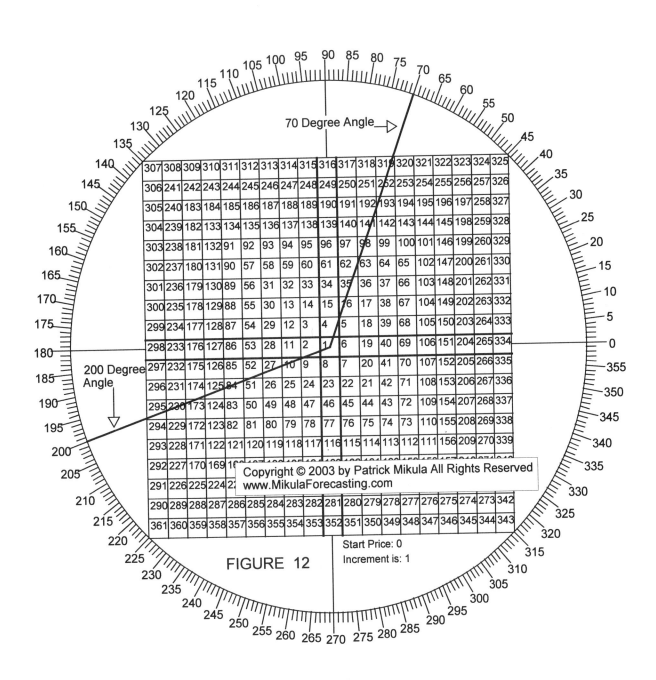

FIGURE 12

W.D.Gann did not always draw the circle around the outside of the Square of Nine because it made the final square very large. The Figure 13 shows how W.D.Gann drew the Square of Nine when the outer circle was not shown. The outer circle's degrees are place at 45° increments around the square.

```
       135°            90°    Figure 13    45°
              ┌──┬──┬──┬──┬──┬──┬──┬──┬───┬───┐
              │91│92│93│94│95│96│97│98│99 │100│101│
              ├──┼──┼──┼──┼──┼──┼──┼──┼───┼───┤
              │90│57│58│59│60│61│62│63│64 │65 │102│
              ├──┼──┼──┼──┼──┼──┼──┼──┼───┼───┤
              │89│56│31│32│33│34│35│36│37 │66 │103│
              ├──┼──┼──┼──┼──┼──┼──┼──┼───┼───┤
              │88│55│30│13│14│15│16│17│38 │67 │104│
              ├──┼──┼──┼──┼──┼──┼──┼──┼───┼───┤
              │87│54│29│12│ 3│ 4│ 5│18│39 │68 │105│
  180°─       ├──┼──┼──┼──┼──┼──┼──┼──┼───┼───┤  ─0°
              │86│53│28│11│ 2│ 1│ 6│19│40 │69 │106│
              ├──┼──┼──┼──┼──┼──┼──┼──┼───┼───┤
              │85│52│27│10│ 9│ 8│ 7│20│41 │70 │107│
              ├──┼──┼──┼──┼──┼──┼──┼──┼───┼───┤
              │84│51│26│25│24│23│22│21│42 │71 │108│
              ├──┼──┼──┼──┼──┼──┼──┼──┼───┼───┤
              │83│50│49│48│47│46│45│44│43 │72 │109│
              ├──┼──┼──┼──┼──┼──┼──┼──┼───┼───┤
              │82│81│80│79│78│77│76│75│74 │73 │110│
              ├──┼──┼──┼──┼──┼──┼──┼──┼───┼───┤
              │121│120│119│118│117│116│115│114│113│112│111│
              └──┴──┴──┴──┴──┴──┴──┴──┴───┴───┘
       225°           270°                 315°
```

The majority of Square of Nine charts W.D.Gann used show the degrees around the outside of the square starting at the center right, labeled A, on Figure 14. There are a few references in W.D.Gann's work to using the center left or bottom left corner for this starting point. These are labeled B and C. In this book, all Square of Nine charts begin from the A position.

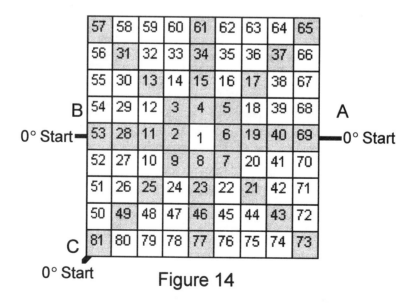

Figure 14

Angle Overlays

There are two types of overlays used with the Square of Nine. These are named: angle overlays and shape overlays. The line diagram in Figure 15 shows the angles from the cardinal cross and diagonal cross. These are <u>fixed</u> angles on the Square of Nine but it is possible to draw these angles on clear plastic to make overlays. The plastic overlay is placed on the Square of Nine and rotated over the Square of Nine. The cardinal cross and diagonal cross identify the numbers on the face of the Square of Nine which are 45° apart. By rotating the overlay, it is possible to see the numbers on the face of the Square of Nine which are 45° apart but from different starting points. The overlay becomes a movable cardinal cross and diagonal cross.

The overlay's 0° angle is always drawn with a heavier line than the other angles. A line on the angle overlay is identified by the number of degrees it is from the 0° angle. For example the line directly opposite the 0° angle is called the overlay's 180° angle. The two lines which are 45° away from the 0° angle are named the overlay's 45° angle and 315° angle. The two lines which are 90° away from the 0° angle are named the overlay's 90° angle and 270° angle.

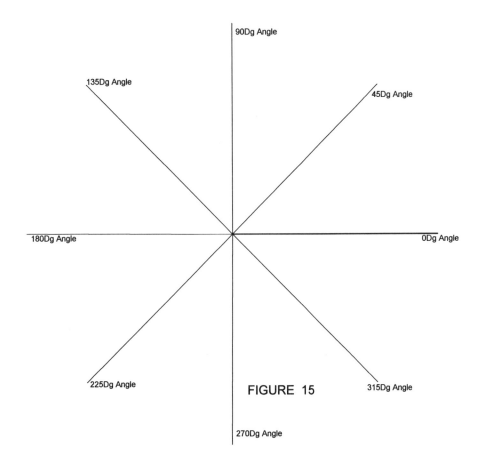

FIGURE 15

The overlay with angles every 45° was not the only overlay W.D.Gann used. The diagram in Figure 16 shows an overlay with an angle every 60°.

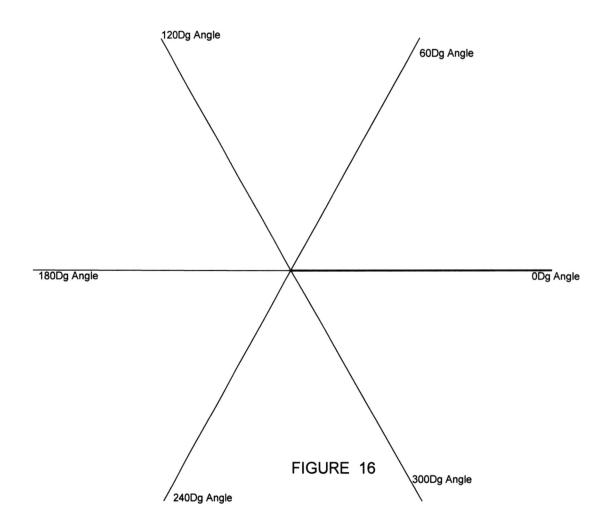

FIGURE 16

The overlay in Figure 17 is a special overlay which W.D.Gann used. This overlay has the 180° angle and two angles which are both 144° from the 0° angle. They are labeled 144 and 216.

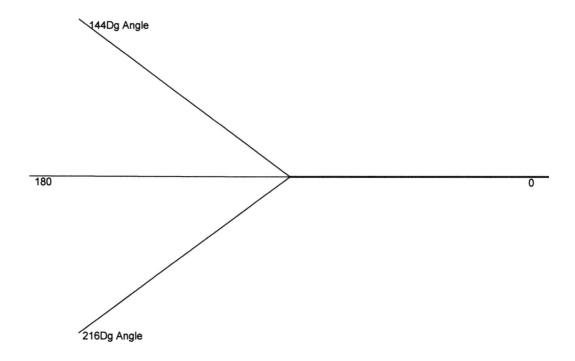

FIGURE 17

Shape Overlays

Geometric shapes are the basis for W.D.Gann's second type of overlays. The two shapes he used are the square and triangle.

On the Square of Nine in Figure 18, there is a triangle overlay. There are two sets of lines on each shape overlay. The first set of lines forms the shape and are heavy, dark lines. The second set of lines are inside the shape and are drawn from the corner of the shape to the center of the Square of Nine. These are fine lines.

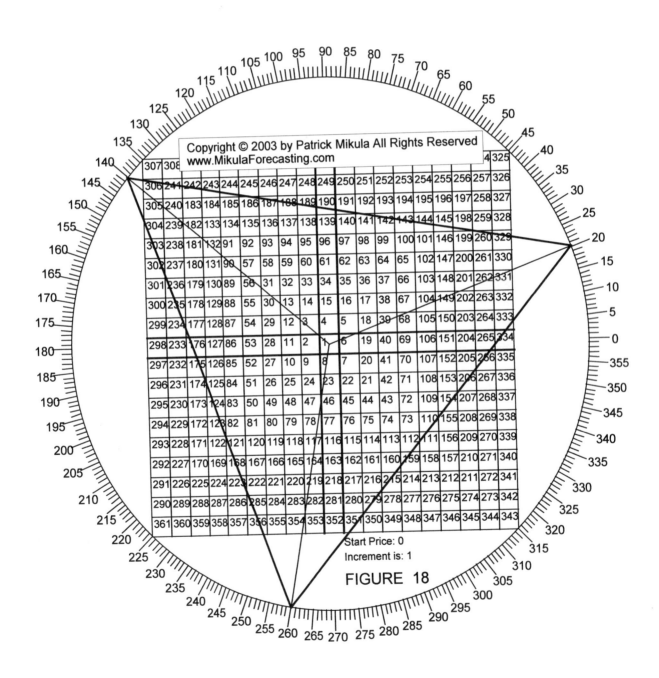

FIGURE 18

Figure 19 shows a Square of Nine with a square shape overlay. Again, there are two sets of lines on this shape overlay. First are the heavy lines which make the square shape. Second are the fine lines which connect each corner to the center of the Square of Nine.

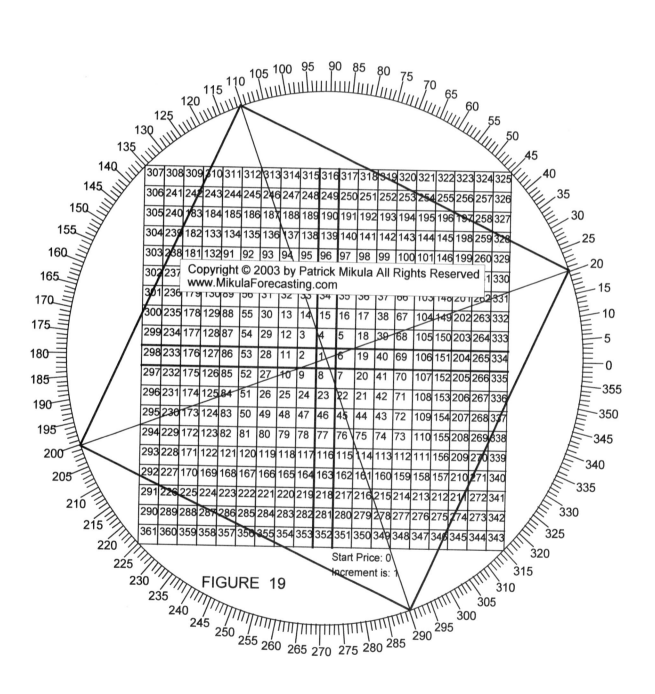

FIGURE 19

Two Ways to Align an Overlay on the Square of Nine

There are two ways to align an overlay on the Square of Nine. The first method is to align the overlay's 0° angle with one of the degree marks on the outer circle of the Square of Nine. On Figure 20, the overlay is rotated so the overlay's 0° angle is aligned on the Square of Nine's outer circle 212° mark. This allows the numbers on the face of the Square of Nine to be seen in 45° increments starting from the 212° mark. For example, the overlay's 0° angle crosses over cells 123, 83, 51-50 and 26. The overlay's 90° angle crosses over cells 159, 113, 75-74, 44 and 22. The overlay's 315° angle crosses over cells 128, 87, 54, 29, and 11-12. This is what is meant by the overlay being a movable cardinal cross and diagonal cross.

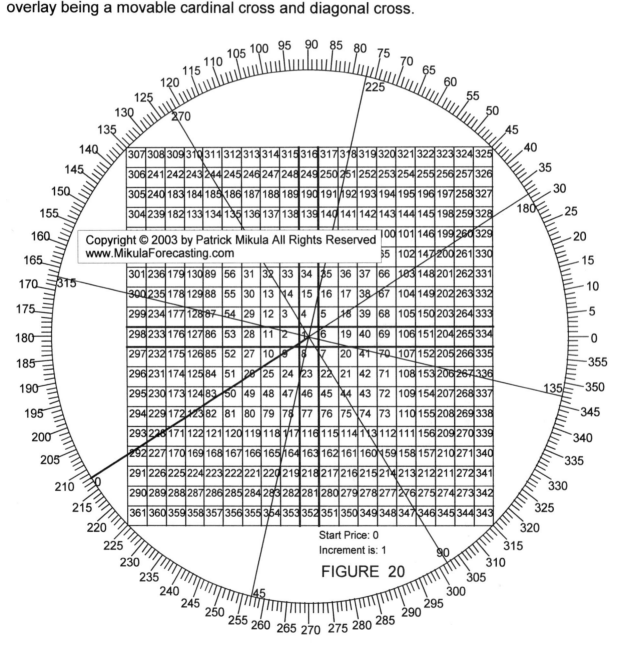

FIGURE 20

The second method for aligning an overlay on the Square of Nine is to place the overlay's 0° angle on top of a cell. On Figure 21, there is an overlay which shows the two angles which are 144° away from the 0° angle. This overlay is aligned so the overlay's 0° angle crosses over cell 154. In this situation it is said that the overlay is aligned to cell 154. When aligning an overlay to a cell, the 0° angle should cross through the center of the cell.

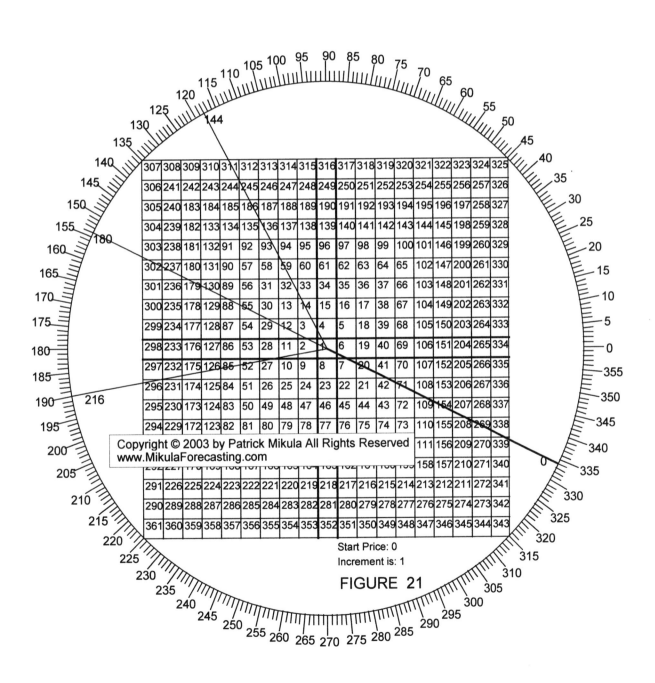

FIGURE 21

A shape overlay is aligned to the Square of Nine using the same two methods used with the angle overlay. With the first method, one of the shape's corners is aligned to a degree mark on the outer circle of the Square of Nine. With the second method, one of the lines which connects the center of the Square of Nine to the shape's corners is aligned to a cell.

Figure 22 shows a triangle overlay. One of the corners of the triangle is aligned to the 20° mark of the outer circle using the first alignment method. Using the second alignment method, one of the lines which connects the center of the Square of Nine to one of the triangle corners is aligned to cell 164.

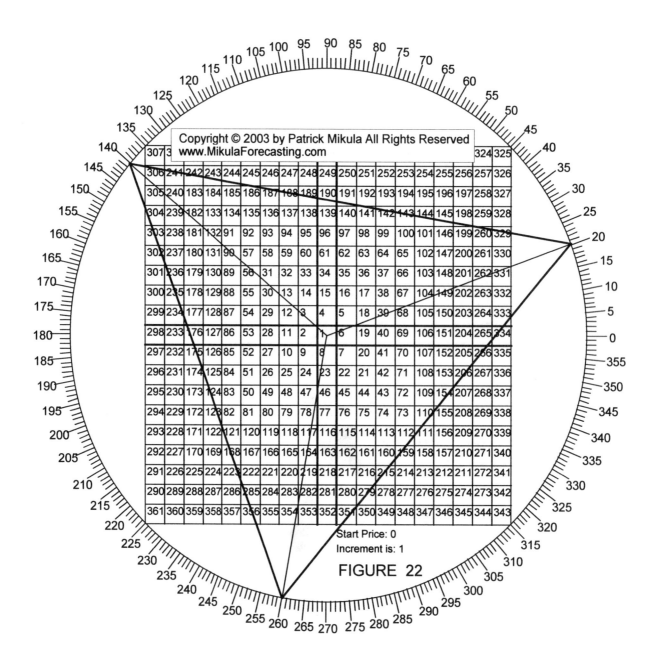

FIGURE 22

The Correct Way to Align an Overlay on a Cell

Stock and futures prices include decimals and do not move by simple whole numbers. To correctly align an overlay to a number such as 37.25 on the Square of Nine, an understanding of how the numbers fit into each cell is required. Figure 23 shows only the upper right section of a Square of Nine. The heavy line is a 45° angle drawn from the center of the Square of Nine in cell 1 to the upper right corner of the square. The 45° angle crosses the center of each cell through which it passes. If lines are drawn along each of the cardinal cross and diagonal cross angles, the lines also bisect each cell through which they pass.

On Figure 23, there are dots marking the prices at increments of 0.25. The prices are also marked with hash marks. A whole number, such as 35, is in the center of cell 35. A whole number, such as 36, is in the center of cell 36. As you move from 35 to 36 the number 35.50 is on the dividing line between cell 35 and cell 36. A difficult part of properly aligning an overlay to a cell, is aligning numbers which have a decimal greater than .5 because these fractions cross into the next cell. For example the price 34.75 is in cell 35, and 35.75 is in cell 36 and so on. If you want to align an overlay to the price 39.75, the overlay would actually be on the top portion of cell 40.

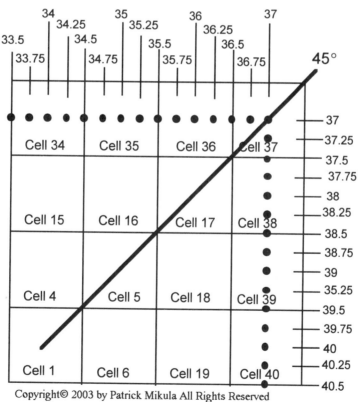

Figure 23

Figure 24 shows the same section of a Square of Nine seen in Figure 23. On Figure 24, there are four new lines drawn through specific prices. The first line runs from the center of the Square of Nine through the price 34.5. This line is drawn at 80.78° and runs directly between cells 34 and 35. The next line runs through the price 36.25. This line is drawn at 53.48° and runs through the right side of cell 36. The next line runs through the price 39. This line runs through the exact center of cell 39 and is 18.43°. The final line is drawn through the price 39.75. This line runs through the top of cell 40 at 4.61°.

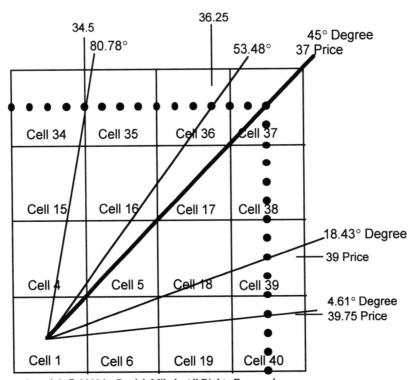

Copyright© 2003 by Patrick Mikula All Rights Reserved
www.MikulaForecasting.com

Figure 24

Angle Degree for Each Cell

Figure 24 shows that the angle drawn from the center of the Square of Nine through cell 39 is draw at 18.43°. When an angle is drawn from the center of the Square of Nine through the center of a cell, the angle's degree can be found with trigonometry. All the relationships between the overlay angles and the numbers on the face of the Square of Nine can be calculated with trigonometry. Providing a chapter on trigonometry is outside the scope of this book so instead, the angle degree which corresponds to each cell up to cell 361 is listed below.

<< Rotation 1 >>
Cell 2 = 180°
Cell 3 = 135°
Cell 4 = 90°
Cell 5 = 45°
Cell 6 = 0°
Cell 7 = 315°
Cell 8 = 270°
Cell 9 = 225°
<< Rotation 2 >>
Cell 10 = 206.56°
Cell 11 = 180°
Cell 12 = 153.43°
Cell 13 = 135°
Cell 14 = 116.56°
Cell 15 = 90°
Cell 16 = 63.43°
Cell 17 = 45°
Cell 18 = 26.56°
Cell 19 = 0°
Cell 20 = 333.43°
Cell 21 = 315°
Cell 22 = 296.56°
Cell 23 = 270°
Cell 24 = 243.43°
Cell 25 = 225°
<< Rotation 3 >>
Cell 26 = 213.69°
Cell 27 = 198.43°
Cell 28 = 180°
Cell 29 = 161.56°
Cell 30 = 146.31°
Cell 31 = 135°
Cell 32 = 123.69°
Cell 33 = 108.43°
Cell 34 = 90°
Cell 35 = 71.56°
Cell 36 = 56.30°
Cell 37 = 45°
Cell 38 = 33.69°
Cell 39 = 18.43°
Cell 40 = 0°
Cell 41 = 341.56°
Cell 42 = 326.31°
Cell 43 = 315°
Cell 44 = 303.69°
Cell 45 = 288.43°
Cell 46 = 270°
Cell 47 = 251.56°
Cell 48 = 236.31°
Cell 49 = 225°
<< Rotation 4 >>
Cell 50 = 216.87°
Cell 51 = 206.56°
Cell 52 = 194.03°
Cell 53 = 180°
Cell 54 = 165.96°
Cell 55 = 153.43°
Cell 56 = 143.13°
Cell 57 = 135°
Cell 58 = 126.87°
Cell 59 = 116.56°
Cell 60 = 104.03°
Cell 61 = 90°
Cell 62 = 75.96°
Cell 63 = 63.43°
Cell 64 = 53.13°
Cell 65 = 45°
Cell 66 = 36.87°
Cell 67 = 26.56°
Cell 68 = 14.03°
Cell 69 = 0°
Cell 70 = 345.96°
Cell 71 = 333.43°
Cell 72 = 323.13°
Cell 73 = 315°
Cell 74 = 306.86°
Cell 75 = 296.56°
Cell 76 = 284.03°
Cell 77 = 270°
Cell 78 = 255.96°
Cell 79 = 243.43°
Cell 80 = 233.13°
Cell 81 = 225°

<< Rotation 5 >>
Cell 82 = 218.65°
Cell 83 = 210.96°
Cell 84 = 201.84°
Cell 85 = 191.31°
Cell 86 = 180°
Cell 87 = 168.69°
Cell 88 = 158.19°
Cell 89 = 149.03°
Cell 90 = 141.34°
Cell 91 = 135°
Cell 92 = 128.65°
Cell 93 = 120.96°
Cell 94 = 111.80°
Cell 95 = 101.30°
Cell 96 = 90°
Cell 97 = 78.69°
Cell 98 = 68.19°
Cell 99 = 59.03°
Cell 100 = 51.34°
Cell 101 = 45°
Cell 102 = 38.65°
Cell 103 = 30.96°
Cell 104 = 21.80°
Cell 105 = 11.31°
Cell 106 = 0°
Cell 107 = 348.69°
Cell 108 = 338.19°
Cell 109 = 329.03°
Cell 110 = 321.34°
Cell 111 = 315°
Cell 112 = 308.65°
Cell 113 = 300.96°
Cell 114 = 291.80°
Cell 115 = 281.30°
Cell 116 = 270°
Cell 117 = 258.69°
Cell 118 = 248.19°
Cell 119 = 239.03°
Cell 120 = 321.34°
Cell 121 = 225°

<< Rotation 6 >>
Cell 122 = 219.80°
Cell 123 = 213.69°
Cell 124 = 206.56°
Cell 125 = 198.43°
Cell 126 = 189.46°
Cell 127 = 180°
Cell 128 = 170.53°
Cell 129 = 161.56°
Cell 130 = 153.43°
Cell 131 = 146.31°
Cell 132 = 140.19°
Cell 133 = 135°
Cell 134 = 129.80°
Cell 135 = 123.69°
Cell 136 = 116.56°
Cell 137 = 108.43°
Cell 138 = 99.46°
Cell 139 = 90°
Cell 140 = 80.53°
Cell 141 = 71.56°
Cell 142 = 63.43°
Cell 143 = 56.31°
Cell 144 = 50.19°
Cell 145 = 45°
Cell 146 = 39.80°
Cell 147 = 33.69°
Cell 148 = 26.56°
Cell 149 = 18.43°
Cell 150 = 9.46°
Cell 151 = 0°
Cell 152 = 350.53°
Cell 153 = 341.56°
Cell 154 = 333.43°
Cell 155 = 326.31°
Cell 156 = 320.19°
Cell 157 = 315°
Cell 158 = 309.80°
Cell 159 = 303.69°
Cell 160 = 296.56°
Cell 161 = 288.43°

Cell 162 = 279.46°
Cell 163 = 270°
Cell 164 = 260.53°
Cell 165 = 251.56°
Cell 166 = 243.43°
Cell 167 = 236.31°
Cell 168 = 230.19°
Cell 169 = 225°

<< Rotation 7 >>
Cell 170 = 220.60°
Cell 171 = 215.53°
Cell 172 = 209.74°
Cell 173 = 203.19°
Cell 174 = 195.94°
Cell 175 = 188.13°
Cell 176 = 180°
Cell 177 = 171.86°
Cell 178 = 164.05°
Cell 179 = 156.80°
Cell 180 = 150.25°
Cell 181 = 144.46°
Cell 182 = 139.39°
Cell 183 = 135°
Cell 184 = 130.60°
Cell 185 = 125.53°
Cell 186 = 119.74°
Cell 187 = 113.19°
Cell 188 = 105.94°
Cell 189 = 98.13°
Cell 190 = 90°
Cell 191 = 81.86°
Cell 192 = 74.05°
Cell 193 = 66.80°
Cell 194 = 60.25°
Cell 195 = 54.46°
Cell 196 = 49.39°
Cell 197 = 45°
Cell 198 = 40.60°
Cell 199 = 35.53°
Cell 200 = 29.74°
Cell 201 = 23.19°

Cell 202 = 15.94°
Cell 203 = 8.13°
Cell 204 = 0°
Cell 205 = 351.87°
Cell 206 = 344.04°
Cell 207 = 336.80°
Cell 208 = 330.25°
Cell 209 = 324.46°
Cell 210 = 319.39°
Cell 211 = 315°
Cell 212 = 310.60°
Cell 213 = 305.53°
Cell 214 = 299.74°
Cell 215 = 293.19°
Cell 216 = 285.94°
Cell 217 = 278.13°
Cell 218 = 270°
Cell 219 = 261.86°
Cell 220 = 254.05°
Cell 221 = 246.80°
Cell 222 = 240.25°
Cell 223 = 234.46°
Cell 224 = 229.39°
Cell 225 = 225°
<< Rotation 8 >>
Cell 226 = 221.18°
Cell 227 = 216.86°
Cell 228 = 212.00°
Cell 229 = 206.56°
Cell 230 = 200.55°
Cell 231 = 194.03°
Cell 232 = 187.12°
Cell 233 = 180°
Cell 234 = 172.87°
Cell 235 = 165.96°
Cell 236 = 159.44°
Cell 237 = 153.43°
Cell 238 = 147.99°
Cell 239 = 143.13°
Cell 240 = 138.81°
Cell 241 = 135°

Cell 242 = 131.18°
Cell 243 = 126.86°
Cell 244 = 122.00°
Cell 245 = 116.56°
Cell 246 = 110.55°
Cell 247 = 104.03°
Cell 248 = 97.12°
Cell 249 = 90°
Cell 250 = 82.87°
Cell 251 = 75.96°
Cell 252 = 69.44°
Cell 253 = 63.43°
Cell 254 = 57.99°
Cell 255 = 53.13°
Cell 256 = 48.81°
Cell 257 = 45°
Cell 258 = 41.18°
Cell 259 = 36.86°
Cell 260 = 32.00°
Cell 261 = 26.56°
Cell 262 = 20.55°
Cell 263 = 14.03°
Cell 264 = 7.12°
Cell 265 = 0°
Cell 266 = 352.87°
Cell 267 = 345.96°
Cell 268 = 339.44°
Cell 269 = 333.43°
Cell 270 = 327.99°
Cell 271 = 323.13°
Cell 272 = 318.81°
Cell 273 = 315°
Cell 274 = 311.18°
Cell 275 = 306.86°
Cell 276 = 302.00°
Cell 277 = 296.56°
Cell 278 = 290.55°
Cell 279 = 284.03°
Cell 280 = 277.12°
Cell 281 = 270°
Cell 282 = 262.87°

Cell 283 = 255.96°
Cell 284 = 249.44°
Cell 285 = 243.43°
Cell 286 = 237.99°
Cell 287 = 233.13°
Cell 288 = 228.81°
Cell 289 = 225°
<< Rotation 9 >>
Cell 290 = 221.63°
Cell 291 = 217.87°
Cell 292 = 213.69°
Cell 293 = 209.05°
Cell 294 = 203.96°
Cell 295 = 198.43°
Cell 296 = 192.52°
Cell 297 = 186.34°
Cell 298 = 180°
Cell 299 = 173.65°
Cell 300 = 167.47°
Cell 301 = 161.56°
Cell 302 = 156.03°
Cell 303 = 150.94°
Cell 304 = 146.31°
Cell 305 = 142.12°
Cell 306 = 138.36°
Cell 307 = 135°
Cell 308 = 131.63°
Cell 309 = 127.87°
Cell 310 = 123.69°
Cell 311 = 119.05°
Cell 312 = 113.96°
Cell 313 = 108.43°
Cell 314 = 102.52°
Cell 315 = 96.34°
Cell 316 = 90°
Cell 317 = 83.65°
Cell 318 = 77.47°
Cell 319 = 71.56°
Cell 320 = 66.03°
Cell 321 = 60.94°
Cell 322 = 56.30°

Cell 323 = 52.12°
Cell 324 = 48.36°
Cell 325 = 45°
Cell 326 = 41.63°
Cell 327 = 37.87°
Cell 328 = 33.69°
Cell 329 = 29.05°
Cell 330 = 23.96°
Cell 331 = 18.43°
Cell 332 = 12.52°
Cell 333 = 6.34°
Cell 334 = 0°
Cell 335 = 353.65°
Cell 336 = 347.47°
Cell 337 = 341.56°
Cell 338 = 336.03°
Cell 339 = 330.94°
Cell 340 = 326.30°
Cell 341 = 322.12°
Cell 342 = 318.36°
Cell 343 = 315°
Cell 344 = 311.63°
Cell 345 = 307.87°
Cell 346 = 303.69°
Cell 347 = 299.05°
Cell 348 = 293.96°
Cell 349 = 288.43°
Cell 350 = 282.52°
Cell 351 = 276.34°
Cell 352 = 270°
Cell 353 = 263.65°
Cell 354 = 257.47°
Cell 355 = 251.56°
Cell 356 = 246.03°
Cell 357 = 240.94°
Cell 358 = 236.30°
Cell 359 = 232.12°
Cell 360 = 228.36°
Cell 361 = 225°

Price Chart Basics

When trades are made in the stock market, there is a record kept of the date, time and price at which the trade was made. Each individual trade is named a tick. Through the course of one day, there may be as few as several hundred ticks in a thinly traded market or many thousands of ticks in a heavily traded market. When making a chart of stock prices, the ticks are grouped into bars. A bar consists of the opening price, high price, low price and closing price. The left tick mark is the opening price. The top of the bar is the high price. The bottom of the bar is the low price and the right tick mark is the closing price. Figure 25 shows a price bar.

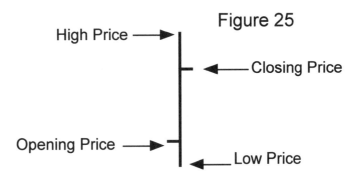

Figure 25

Figure 26 shows a price bar chart for a stock. On the left edge is the Y axis which holds the price scale. Across the bottom is the X axis which holds the time scale.

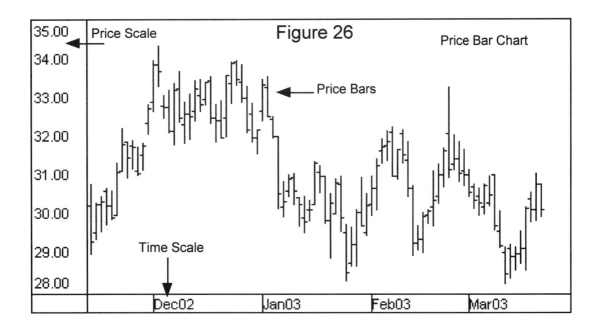

Figure 26

Defining Pivots

This book uses the terms pivot, pivot price, pivot bar and pivot point. A pivot is the location on the chart at which the price stops moving in one direction and starts moving in the opposite direction. Figure 27 has an arrow labeled Pivot Price. This identifies the price where the stock stopped moving up and turned downward. The label, Pivot Bar, identifies the bar on which the stock stopped moving upward and turned downward. The pivot price and pivot bar together make the pivot point. There can be a top pivot and bottom pivot.

Defining Support and Resistance Lines

When the price moves up and finds selling resistance which prevents the price from moving any higher, this price level is named a resistance level. On Figure 27 there is a horizontal line labeled, Price Resistance Level. When the price moves up to this line, there is selling resistance to the market moving up any further.

When the price falls and finds buying support which stops the price from falling further, that price level is named a support level. On Figure 27, there is a horizontal line labeled Price Support Level. When the price moves down to the support level, it finds buying support and is prevented from falling any further.

Defining a Congestion Area

Some times the price bars move in a sideways pattern and cover only a small price range. When the price moves sideways, this is named a congestion area. Figure 27 shows a sideways congestion area.

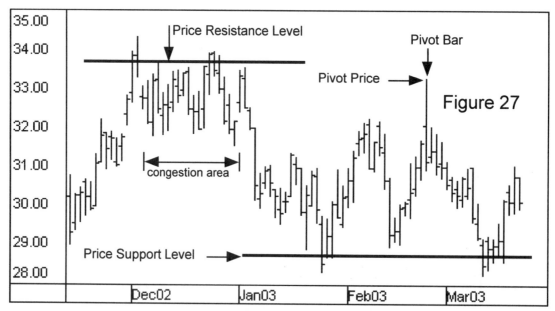

Figure 27

CHAPTER 2: Forecasting Prices:
Using Cell Numbers

This chapter shows how to forecast support an resistance price levels using the cell numbers on the Square of Nine

Example 1 - Weekly S&P500

One of the hardest concepts for traders to grasp is how the numbers on the face of the Square of Nine are used as stock prices. This example shows how to convert the cell numbers on the Square of Nine diagonal cross and cardinal cross into support and resistance price levels. Figure 28 shows a weekly bar chart for the S&P500. The numbers 1030 to 1600 on the chart's left side are the price scale.

W.D.Gann said that markets have their own personality. This is illustrated by the fact that most of the pivots which a market forms are located near price levels from one or two Square of Nine angles. Figure 28 shows the cell numbers from the Square of Nine 225° angle drawn on the chart as support and resistance lines. The 225° angle is the downward left angle in the diagonal cross. The left end of each line is labeled, 225Dg, which is the Square of Nine degree. The right end of each line shows the cell number. On Figure 28 the letters A, B, C, D, E and F mark a pivot near a 225° support and resistance line. This indicates the market favors the 225° angle. When a market favors an angle, that angle can be used to forecast support and resistance. The recent past will often be the best predictor of the near future.

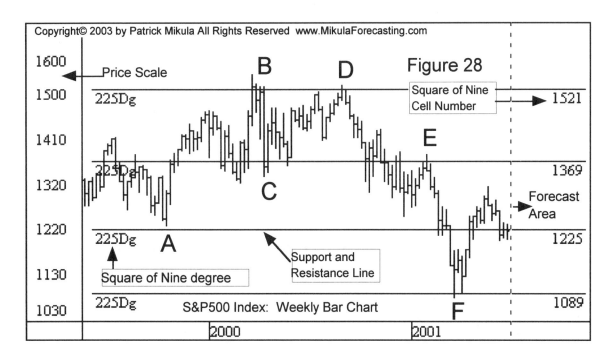

Figure 29 shows the lower left section of the Square of Nine. The cells along the 225° angle are circled. These are the cell numbers which are used as support and resistance level on Figure 28 and 30.

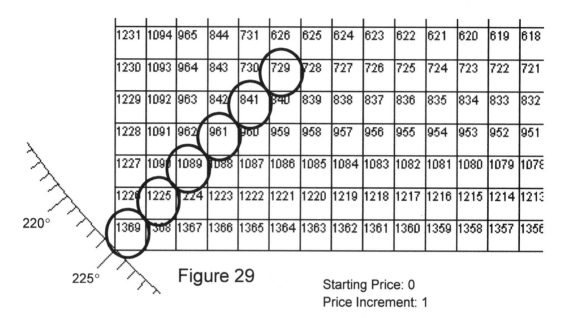

Figure 29

Starting Price: 0
Price Increment: 1

Figure 30 is a continuation of the chart seen in Figure 28. Because the S&P500 favors the 225° angle, more pivots are expected to form against this angle's support and resistance lines. After point F on Figure 30, this market does form the pivots at point G, H, I and J. The pivots G to J form near the support and resistance lines from the 225° angle.

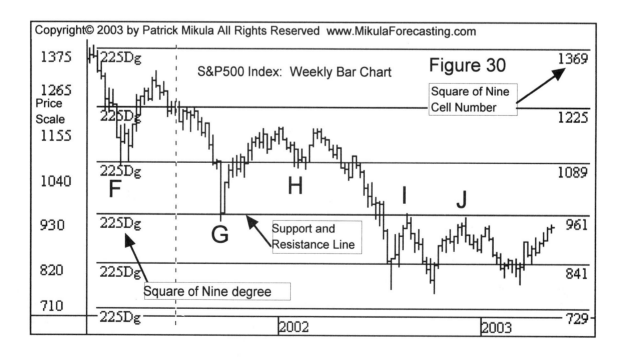

Example 2 of Forecasting Prices Using Cell Numbers:
Daily Live Cattle

Traders frequently question how the Square of Nine can be applied to a stock or future which has a low price range. The answer is that the cell numbers on the Square of Nine are divided by 10 or 100 to generate lower price values. Figure 31 shows a Live Cattle futures chart with a price range from 67 to 73.

The Square of Nine in Figure 32 corresponds to the Figure 31 Live Cattle chart. The Square of Nine in Figure 32 has a circle around cell number 677 on the 45° angle. To use this Square of Nine value on the cattle chart, 677 is divided by 10. This provides a support and resistance price level of 67.7. On Figure 31, there is a heavy horizontal line across the bottom of the chart. The text, 45Dg, is on the left side of the line and the text, 67.7, is on the right side of the line. This Live Cattle market makes a bottom pivot against this support and resistance level at point A.

Figure 32 also has a circle around cell number 729 on the 225° angle. To use this Square of Nine cell number on the Live Cattle chart, 729 is divided by 10. This provides a support and resistance price level of 72.9. On Figure 31, there is a heavy horizontal line across the top of the chart. The text, 225Dg appears on the left side of the line. This refers to the angle on the Square of Nine. On the right side of the line is the text, 72.9. This is the Square of Nine cell number. Figure 31 shows a top pivot near this support and resistance level at point B and C.

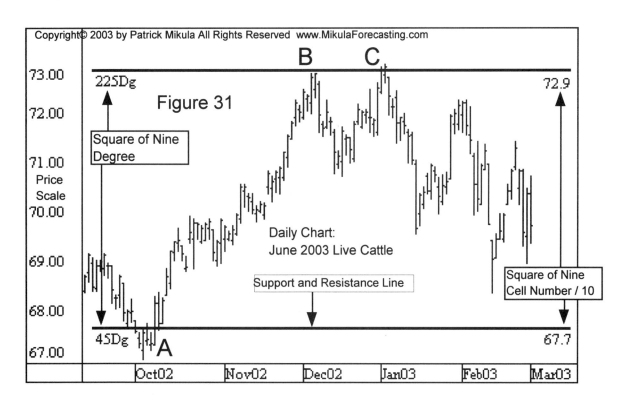

Figure 32 shows the Square of Nine which corresponds with the Figure 31 Live Cattle chart. There are circles around cell 677 on the 45° angle and cell 729 on the 225° angle. These two cell numbers provide support and resistance in the Live Cattle market.

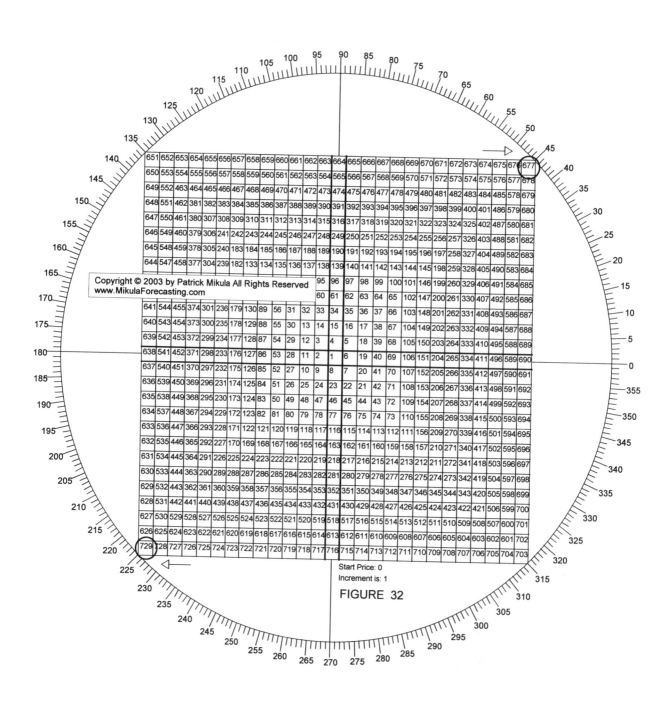

FIGURE 32

Example 3 of Forecasting Prices Using Cell Numbers:
Daily Euro Currency

Figure 33 shows a chart for the Euro Currency. This chart has a very low price scale running from 0.93 to 1.03. The Square of Nine in Figure 34 corresponds to this chart.

To use the cell numbers from the Square of Nine as support and resistance levels on this chart, the cell numbers are divided by 100. There are only two cell numbers on the diagonal cross and cardinal cross which fall in this chart's price range. The first cell number is 101 on the 45° angle and becomes 1.01 when divided by 100. The second cell number is 96 on the 90° angle and becomes 0.96 when divided by 100.

On Figure 33, the top support and resistance line has the text, 45Dg, on the left end of the line. The text, 1.01, appears on the right end of the line. This indicates the line is from a cell on the 45° angle and is drawn at the price 1.01. The bottom support and resistance line has the text, 90Dg, on the left. The text, 0.96, is on the right end of the line. Therefore, this line is based on a cell number from the 90° angle and is drawn at the price 0.96.

The market forms a top pivot when it touches the 1.01 support and resistance line at point A. The market then forms a bottom pivot when it hits the 0.96 support and resistance line at point B and C. This shows the market favors the support and resistance price levels from the 45° angle and the 90° angle. After a market shows it favors an angle, the support and resistance levels from that angle can be used to forecast support and resistance prices.

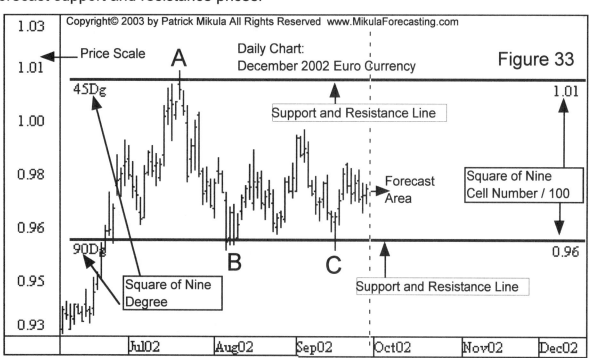

Figure 34 shows the Square of Nine that accompanies the Figure 33 Euro Currency chart. There are hundreds of economic variables which go into determining the value of a currency. Over the time period seen in Figure 33, a lot of unfavorable economic news in the U.S. drove the swings in the Euro Currency. During this time, the Square of Nine performed well in defining the important support and resistance levels. On Figure 34, there are circles around cells 101 and 96. These cells are used for support and resistance levels.

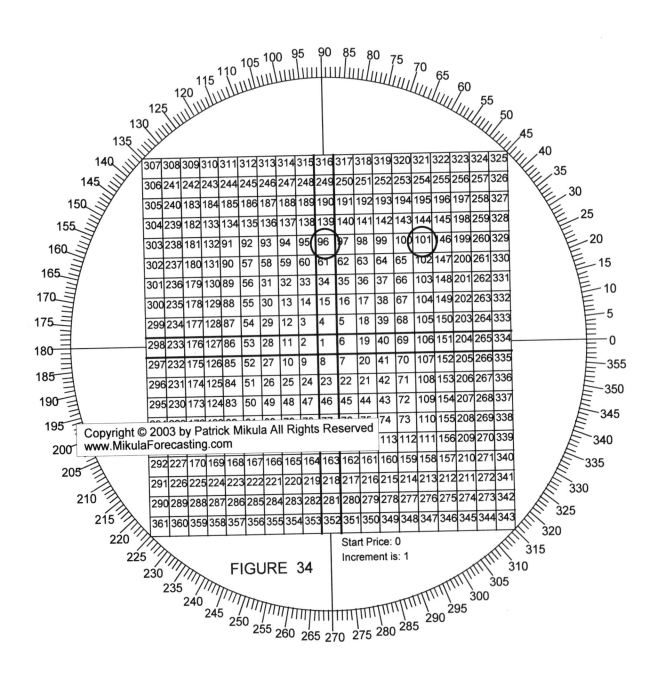

FIGURE 34

Figure 35 is a continuation of the chart in Figure 33. The Euro Currency shows that it favors the support and resistance levels from the 45° angle and the 90° angle. This market is expected to produce more pivots near these support and resistance levels. The best forecaster of the near future is the recent past. After the bottom at point C, the Euro Currency market moves up and makes another top pivot at point D.

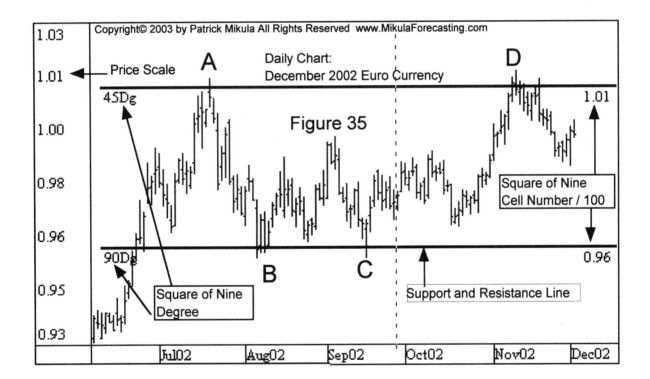

Example 4 of Forecasting Prices Using Cell Numbers: Daily DJIA

Here is one more variation on forecasting prices using cell numbers. This example uses two price charts and no Square of Nine because the chart's price scale is very high. Figure 36 shows the Dow Jones Industrial Average. The cell numbers from the Square of Nine 225° angle and the 45° angle are used to create the support and resistance lines. The price scale is on the far left of the chart and runs from 7195 to 9045. This is a very high price scale. The support and resistance lines are drawn across the chart. The Square of Nine cell numbers which are used as the support and resistance prices are listed on the right edge of the support and resistance lines. The degrees on the Square of Nine, where the cells are located, are written on the left edge of the support and resistance lines. These are identified with the text, 225Dg, and, 45Dg.

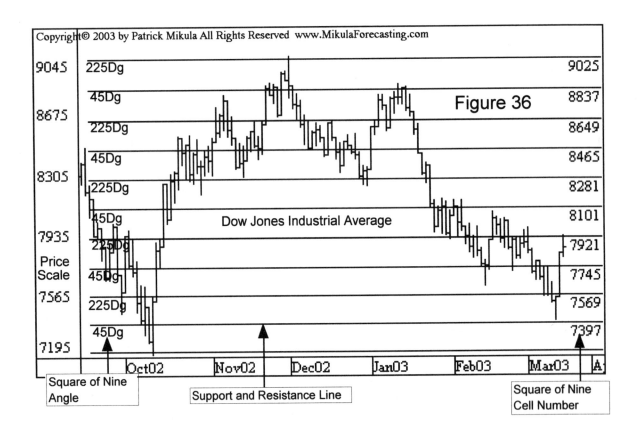

To forecast prices using cell numbers when there is a very high price scale, the decimal place in the price data is moved one place to the left in order to reduce the number of cells required. This is done when a trader does not want to use a Square of Nine which goes up into the thousands.

Figure 37 shows the same DJIA chart as Figure 36, but now the information is plotted after the prices are <u>divided by 10</u>. To chart the cell number that is used as support and resistance, the cell number is <u>multiplied by 10</u>. This increases the cell number and allows it to be drawn on the chart. The support and resistance price for each line is on the right side of Figure 37. The top support and resistance price is 9010. This means the cell number from the Square of Nine is 901. This cell number is multiplied by 10 to create the price 9010.

The highest Square of Nine cell needed to apply this technique to the chart on Figure 37 is 901. Cell numbers up to 9025 are required to apply this method on Figure 36.

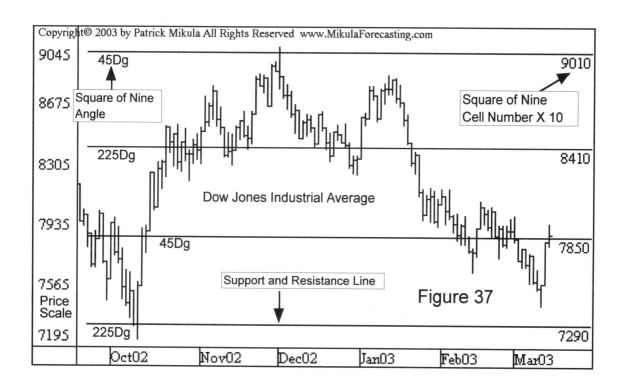

Chapter 2 Review

Objective:
Forecast support and resistance levels using the cell numbers from the Square of Nine cardinal cross and diagonal cross.

Step 1:
The Square of Nine cell numbers from the cardinal cross and diagonal cross are drawn on a price chart as support and resistance lines.

Step 2:
Each market has its own tendency and favors one or two of the cardinal cross and diagonal cross angles. Pivots form around support and resistance lines which a market favors. Select the cardinal cross and diagonal cross angles which the market seems to prefer. Then draw support and resistance lines from these angles on the price chart. Use the angles which the market seems to favor to forecast support and resistance.

Step 3:
Use the support and resistance lines drawn in step 2 to forecast price levels where future pivots are expected to occur. The best indication of the near future is the recent past. When a pivot forms around a support and resistance line, it should be watched in the near future for another pivot to form around the same line. Any line which provided support in the past can be expected to provide resistance in the future. The opposite is also true. It can be expected that a line which provided resistance in the past, will provide support in the future.

CHAPTER 3: Forecasting Price: Using Overlays and Cell Numbers

This chapter shows how to forecast support and resistance price levels using the Square of Nine cell numbers and overlays

Example 1 - Daily Crude Oil

This example of using overlays and cell numbers uses the daily Crude Oil chart in Figure 38 and the Square of Nine in Figure 39. The Crude Oil market had a large run up in 2002-2003. Figure 38 shows how the June 2003 Crude Oil contract forms a pivot bottom on 11/13/2002 at a price of 23.40. On Figure 39 the overlay's 0° angle is aligned on the low price 23.40. The next higher price from the overlay's 180° angle is drawn as a support and resistance line on Figure 38. This price is 34.58 and is circled on the Square of Nine. The letter A marks the point where price bars touch this support and resistance line.

When the Square of Nine overlay is aligned on a significant pivot, it is common to have future pivots occur on the prices identified by the overlay's angles. In this example, the Crude Oil bull market moves 180° around the Square of Nine from bottom to top.

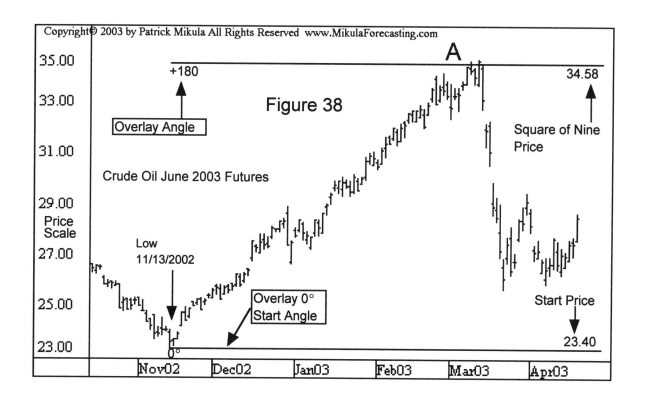

Figure 39 shows the overlay's 0° angle aligned on 23.40. This is the low pivot price from the Crude Oil chart and is circled on Figure 39. The price which is 180° higher on the Square of Nine, is 34.58. This number is also circled on the Square of Nine. This 180° movement represents the low to high range of the Crude Oil up swing.

The Square of Nine successfully defines market price swings but it does not make the market form pivots. At point A on Figure 38, a belief that the U.S. would quickly win its war against Iraq swept through the oil market. When this happened, the Crude Oil price was right on top this Square of Nine support and resistance level and the price collapsed.

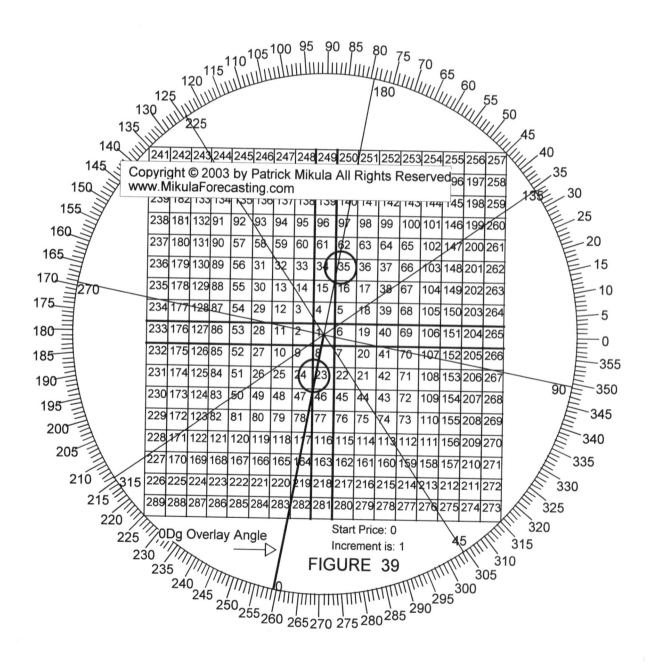

FIGURE 39

Example 2 of Forecasting Price Using Cell Numbers and Overlays: Daily Coffee

When forecasting prices using the Square of Nine and an overlay, W.D.Gann's belief that markets have their own personality is important. Using the overlay, a market's price swings are measured by the number of degrees around the Square of Nine the price travels. A market often favors an amount of movement around the Square of Nine when forming price swings. For example, a market may have a lot of price swings which are approximately 90° or 120° of movement around the Square of Nine. A market's swings are measured from low to high, high to low, low to low and high to high. When the number of degrees of movement that a market favors is found, that information can be used to make a price forecast.

Figure 40 shows a bar chart for July 2003 Coffee futures. From the bottom at point A, to the higher bottom at point C, there are approximately +45° of price movement on the Square of Nine. From the top at point B to the lower top at point D, there are approximately -45° of price movement . From the bottom at point C to the lower bottom at point E, there are approximately -45° of price movement on the Square of Nine. This shows the July Coffee contract favors a distance of +-45° of price movement from high to high or low to low.

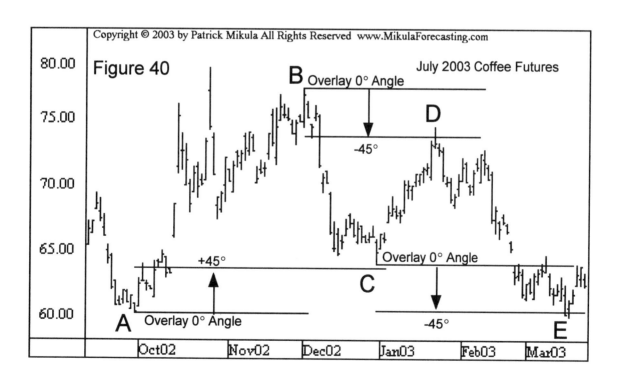

Figure 41 shows the Coffee chart with a price forecast for the next top after point D. The forecast price is -45° from the top price at point D on the Square of Nine.

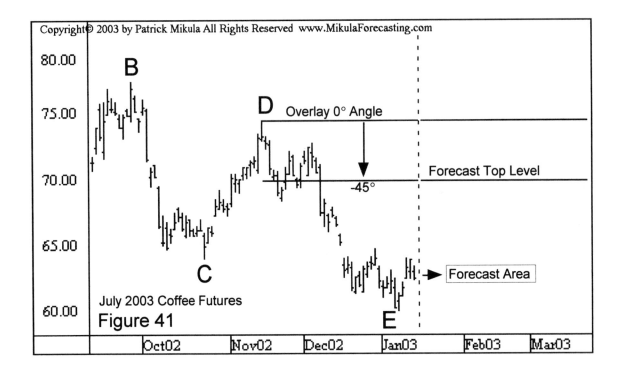

Figure 42 shows the Square of Nine for the forecast in Figure 41. The overlay's 0° angle is aligned on the top price from point D which is 74.50. This starting price is circled. The price of 70, which is -45° from the starting price, is also circled. This is identified by the 45° angle which crosses over it. The circled cell number on the overlay's 45° angle is 70 but the actual value at -45° is 69.95. The forecast top in Figure 41 is set at the price 69.95.

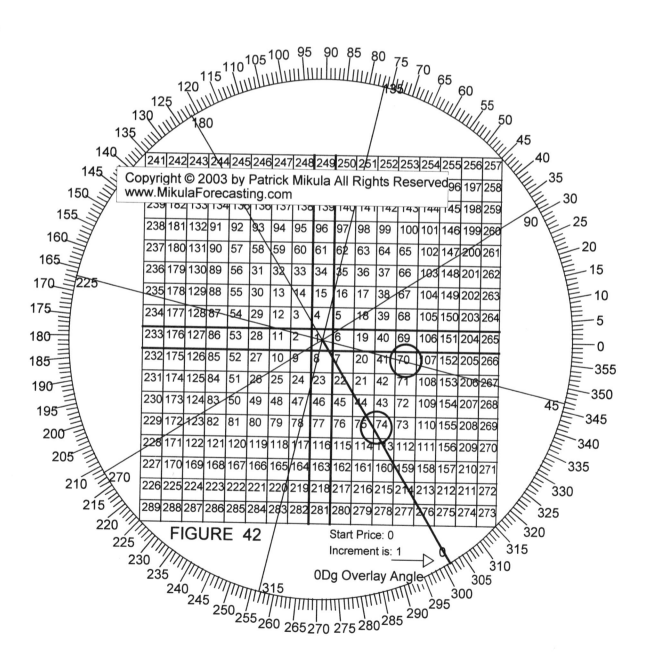

FIGURE 42

Figure 43 shows that after the bottom at point E, the price moves up to the forecast top price level and makes a top at point F. This means the price continues to favor a +-45° difference between tops. By constantly measuring a market's price swings and finding the amount of movement which the market favors, it is possible to forecast top and bottom price levels on an ongoing basis.

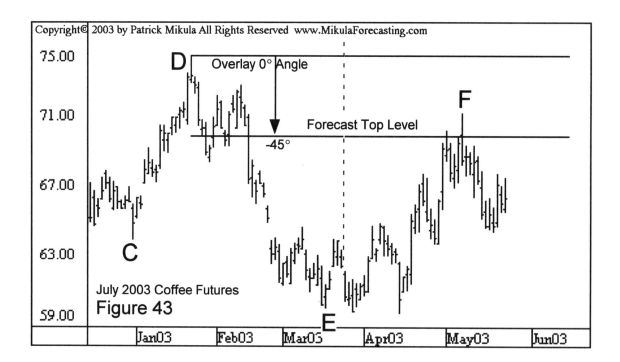

Example 3 of Forecasting Price Using Cell Numbers and Overlays:
Daily Gateway 2000, GTW

The next example uses the stock for Gateway 2000 Inc. symbol GTW. Gateway is a company that sells desktop computers to the public. On Figure 44, the recent pivot top 4.45 on 11/08/2002 is used as the starting price for the overlay's 0° angle. The price 4.45 is too low to use with the Square of Nine so this price is multiplied by 10 to create the price 44.5. On Figure 45, the overlay's 0° angle is aligned to the price 44.5, which is circled. Starting from 44.5, the price of 22 is -360° inward to the center of the square. This price is also circled on the Square of Nine. To use the price 22 on the Gateway chart, it is divided by 10 to reduce the price to the original price scale. The price 22 becomes 2.20 and is drawn on Figure 44 as a support line.

The previous example describes measuring a market's price swings to find the amount of movement, in degrees, that a market favors. Price movements of 180° and 360° on the Square of Nine, show up in the markets so frequently, they always can be used as support and resistance levels.

The price of Gateway 2000 falls from the top at 4.45 down to the -360° support and resistance line. There, the price finds support and moves sideways along this line for a few months. This is identified by the letters A and B which mark the area where the price moves sideways along this support line.

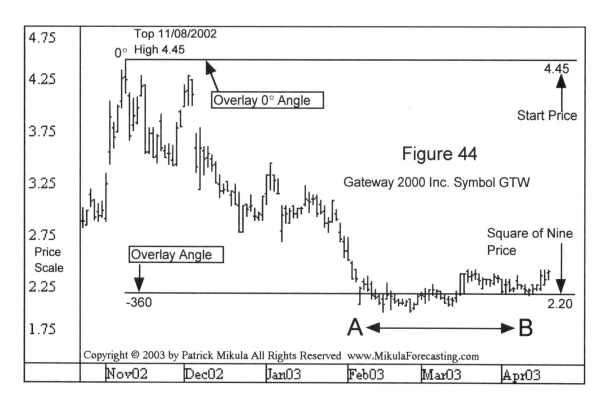

The Square of Nine in Figure 45 shows the overlay's 0° angle aligned to the price 44.5. The price of 22 is 360° inward to the center of the square. This shows the price move from 4.45 to 2.20 in Gateway 2000 stock, is a move of -360° on the Square of Nine. It is common to see a stock make a swing from high to low which is 360° around the Square of Nine. There often is some market news which stops a price advance or decline very near the Square of Nine support line. In this example, when the price of Gateway fell to the -360° support line seen in Figure 44, the biggest companies in the retail computer sector such as DELL and Hewlett-Packard made an announcement. They believed computer sales would increase for the next two quarters. This supported the Gateway stock price and stopped the decline.

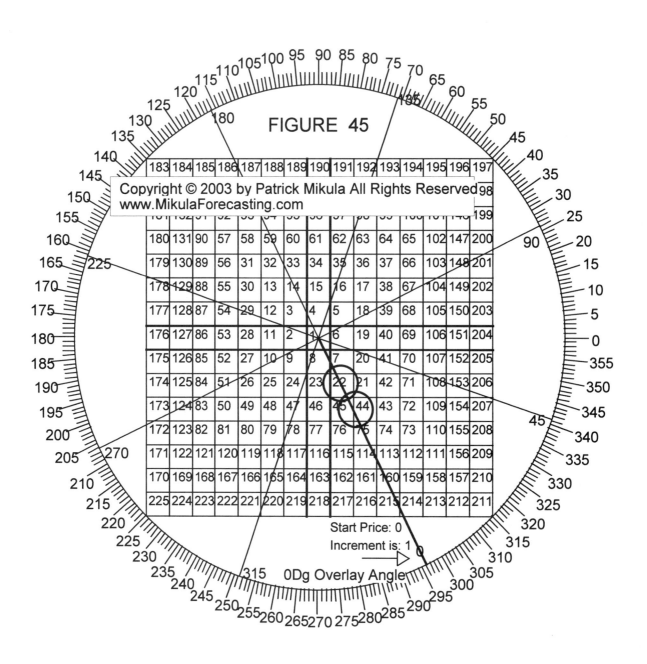

FIGURE 45

Example 4 of Forecasting Price Using Cell Numbers and Overlays:
Daily Japanese Yen

Figure 46 shows a chart for the June 2003 Japanese Yen contract. The price scale for the Yen is frequently presented as a decimal followed by four digits such as .8620. This type of price is far too low to work with the Square of Nine so the scale on this chart is multiplied by 1000. In this case the price .8620 becomes 862.0. The higher prices allow the Square of Nine to be used for forecasting the Japanese Yen.

The first step is to measure the market's price swings and look for an amount of movement on the Square of Nine which the market seems to favor. Figure 46 shows the basic measurements for the price swings in the Japanese Yen.

From the top at point A, to the bottom at point B, the price moves approximately -90°.
From the bottom at point B, to the top at point C, the price moves approximately +120°.
From the top at point C, to the bottom at point D, the price moves approximately -120°.
From the bottom at point D, to the top at point E, the price moves approximately +90°.
From the top at point E, to the bottom at point F, the price moves approximately -60°.

The sequence of movements is -90°, +120°, -120°, +90°, and -60°. This shows the market favors price movements in increments of 90° and 120°. Figure 46 shows the forecast price levels for the next top after point F. The price levels are +90° and +120° up from the bottom at point F.

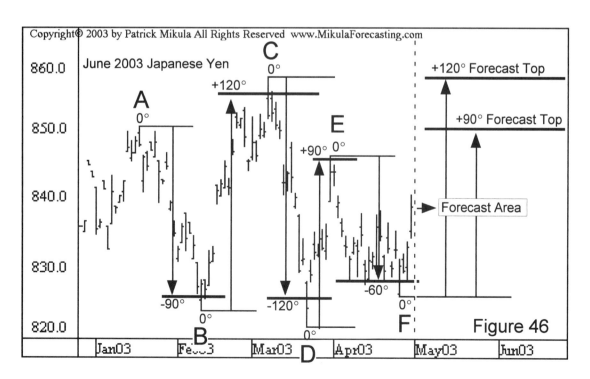

Figure 46

Figure 47 is the Square of Nine for the Japanese Yen forecast in Figure 46. The overlay's 0° angle is aligned on the bottom price from point F which is 826.9. There are also circles around the forecast price 855.9 which is +90° and the forecast price 864.50 which is +120°.

The price 855.9, which is +90° from the starting price of 826.9, is located on the overlay's 270° angle and not the overlay's 90° angle. This is because the overlay's angles are numbered counter clockwise like the degrees on the Square of Nine's outer circle; however, the numbers on the face of the Square of Nine move clockwise. This means the prices which are +90° higher than a starting price are on the overlay's 270° angle. The prices that are -90° lower than a starting price are on the overlay's 90° angle. The same is true for the forecast price which is +120° higher than the starting price. This +120° forecast price is located on the overlay's 240° angle. This is shown on Figure 47.

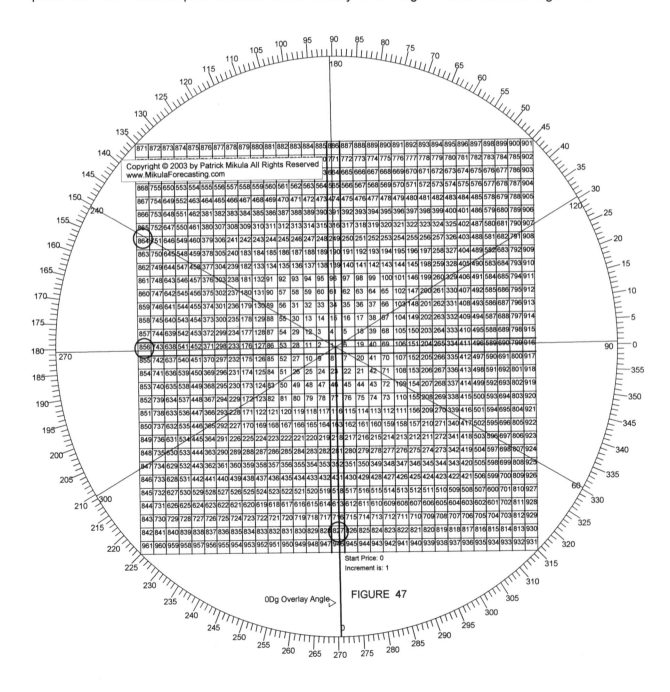

FIGURE 47

Figure 48 shows the Japanese Yen chart with the upward price swing after the bottom pivot F. The price moves up and forms a top at point G against the +120° price forecast.

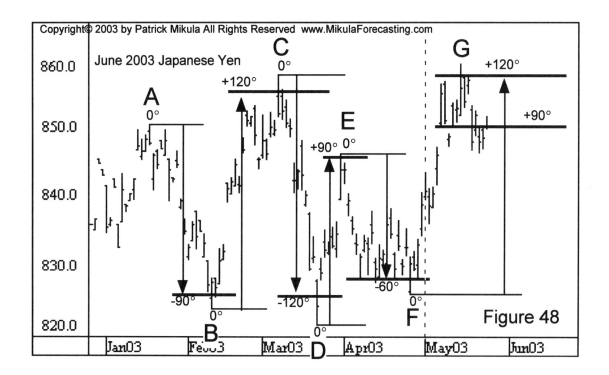

Chapter 3 Review

Objective:
Forecast support and resistance levels based on prices identified by overlay angles.

Step 1:
Measure the market's price swings in degrees using the overlay and the Square of Nine. Price swings are measured from high to high, low to low, high to low and low to high. Using the overlay, look for increments of movement which a market favors. This is the increment of movement which occurs frequently in a market. The standard increments in degrees found on the overlay are 45°, 60°, 90°, 180° and 360°.

Step 2:
Select a starting price on which to align the overlay's 0° angle on the Square of Nine. This usually is a pivot price.

Step 3:
Align the overlay's 0° angle to the starting price on the Square of Nine. If the starting price is very low, multiply the price by 10, 100 or 1000 to create a higher price to use with the Square of Nine. If the starting price is very high, divide it by 10 or 100 to reduce the starting price.

Step 4:
The angles on the overlay cross over prices on the Square of Nine. These prices are used to forecast support and resistance prices. Future top and bottom pivots often occur on the prices identified by the overlay.

CHAPTER 4: Forecasting Dates: Using Cell Numbers

This chapter shows how to forecast pivot dates using Square of Nine cell numbers

Example 1 - Weekly S&P500

This example uses the cell numbers from the Square of Nine diagonal cross and cardinal cross to locate future dates where pivots might occur. Figure 49 shows a weekly chart for the S&P500.

The first step is to select a top or bottom pivot date to use as the starting date. This example uses the pivot bottom date March 23, 2001 as the starting date.

The second step is to count forward from the starting bar, a number of bars equal to the cell numbers on the diagonal cross and cardinal cross and add hash marks. On Figure 49, this is done for the diagonal cross 225° angle. There are hash marks and cell numbers on Figure 49 for the bars which are 9, 25, 49 and 81 bars past the starting bar.

The third step is to study the first two or three hash marks from each count to determine if one of the counts correlates with market pivots. If a correlation is found, the count is used for forecasting. On Figure 49, the first two values from the Square of Nine 225° angle count correlate with market pivots. The value 9 correlates with a top and the value 25 correlates with a bottom.

The fourth step is to use the count found in step 3 and mark the count's future dates on the chart. On Figure 49, the cell numbers 49 and 81 are marked in the forecast area of the chart. There are two pieces of information which are obtained and forecast with the technique. The first piece of information is the future date, which is a pivot date forecast. The second piece of information is whether the pivot will be a top or bottom. To determine if a forecast pivot date will be a top or bottom requires the pivots which come before the forecast date to stay in a top, bottom, top bottom sequence.

For example, on Figure 49, cell number 9 correlates with a top and cell number 25 correlates with a bottom. This top - bottom sequence allows us to forecast that the next pivot at 49 will be a top and the pivot after that, at 81, will be a bottom. If there is no top - bottom sequence, only the pivot date will be forecast. For example, if cells number 9 and 25 both correlated with tops, the pivot date at 49 can still be forecast but there will be no forecast for it to be a top or a bottom.

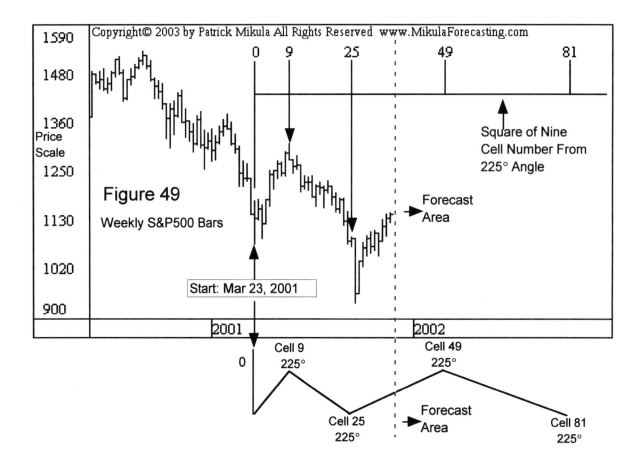

Figure 49 — Weekly S&P500 Bars

One important note; Notice that the hash mark for cell number 25 comes one bar before the actual bottom week with which it correlates. When dealing with only one pivot, it is possible to find an exact match between the cell number date and the market pivot date. When dealing with multiple cell number dates, there seldom is an exact match. If two cell number dates can be found to correlate with market pivots within +-1 bar, that is considered accurate. If three cell number dates can be found to correlate with market pivots within +-2 bars, that is an accurate match. Do not expect to see a sequence of multiple pivots which correlate exactly to cell number dates, that is extremely rare.

The line diagram across the bottom of Figure 49 shows the forecast for the pivot dates and the forecast for the top - bottom sequence.

The Square of Nine in Figure 50 accompanies the chart in Figure 49. The starting date is listed at the bottom of the square as Fri/03/23/01. The dates on this Square of Nine advance 1 week per cell because the S&P500 price chart is a weekly chart. The circles along the 225° angle represent the actual pivot dates in the S&P500. The dates on the 225° angle are seen in MM/DD/YY format. The date in cell 9 is 05/25/01. The date in cell 25 is 09/14/01. The date in cell 49 is 03/01/02. The date in cell 81 is 10/11/02 and in cell 121 is 07/18/03.

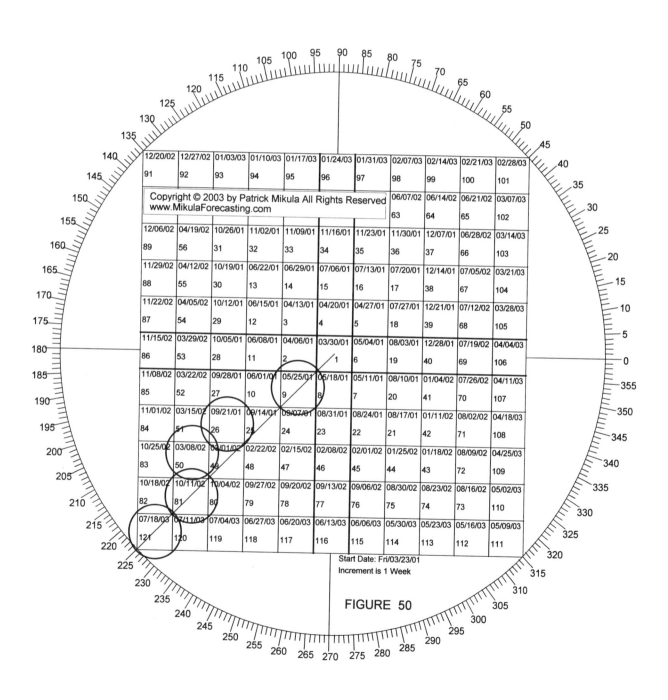

FIGURE 50

Figure 51 shows the continuation of the S&P500 weekly chart. After the pivot bottom which correlates with cell number 25, the S&P500 moves up and forms a flat top near the hash mark for cell 49. The market then falls and makes a sharp bottom exactly on the date identified by the hash mark for cell 81. The next forecast move is an up swing until the date identified by the hash mark for cell 121.

W.D.Gann believed that an original market impulse works itself out into rhythmic market movements. The starting pivot in this technique functions as the original impulse. The date count from the Square of Nine allows a forecast of the resulting rhythmic movements.

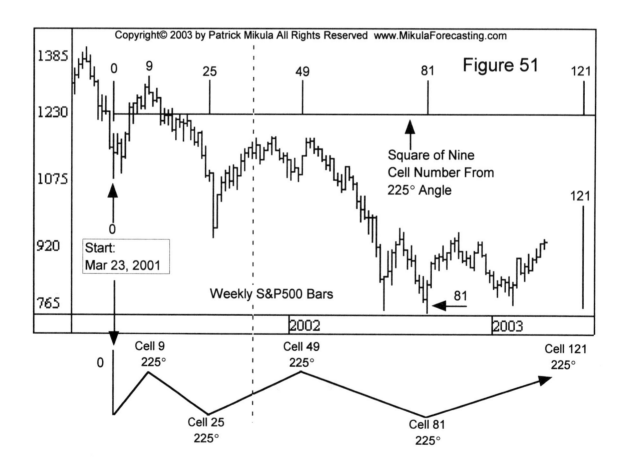

Example 2 of Forecasting Dates with Cell Numbers:
Daily Altera, ALTR

Figure 52 shows a daily bar chart for the semiconductor company Altera, symbol ALTR. When using a daily chart, each cell on the Square of Nine is counted in calendar days or trading days. On Figure 52, the low pivot date October 8, 2002 is used as the starting date. Along the bottom of the bar chart is a horizontal line with vertical hash marks extending above and below it. These vertical hash marks are labeled with the cell numbers 17, 37, 65 and 101 from the Square of Nine, 45° angle. The count for calendar days is shown above the horizontal line and the count for trading days is below the horizontal line.

Using two counts is more difficult than using only one count. After selecting a starting point, the angles from the Square of Nine are selected based on their ability to correlate with market pivots. In this example, the 45° angle is selected from both the calender count Square of Nine and the trading count Square of Nine. The count values which correlate with a market pivot are circled. Not all the values from both counts correlate with pivots. After finding the Square of Nine angle which correlates with two or three pivots in a row, the next step is to forecast the next probable pivot dates. On Figure 52, the forecast dates are identified by the hash marks for calender days 65 and 101 and the trading day 65 hash mark.

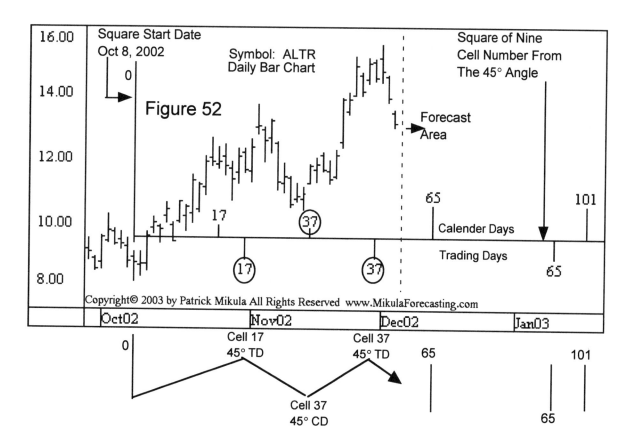

The Square of Nine in Figure 53 accompanies the Figure 52 chart. The starting date, Tue/October/08/2002, is at the bottom of the Square of Nine. This start date is the pivot low date from the Figure 52 bar chart. The dates on this Square of Nine advance by 1 <u>trading day</u>. Figure 52 shows the trading days count using the cell numbers from the Square of Nine 45° angle as 17, 37, 65 and 101. These cells are circled on the 45° angle below. The dates are in MM/DD/YY format. On the Square of Nine in Figure 53, cell 17 represents 10/31/02. Cell 37 represents 11/28/02. Cell 65 represents 01/07/03. Cell 101 represents 02/26/03.

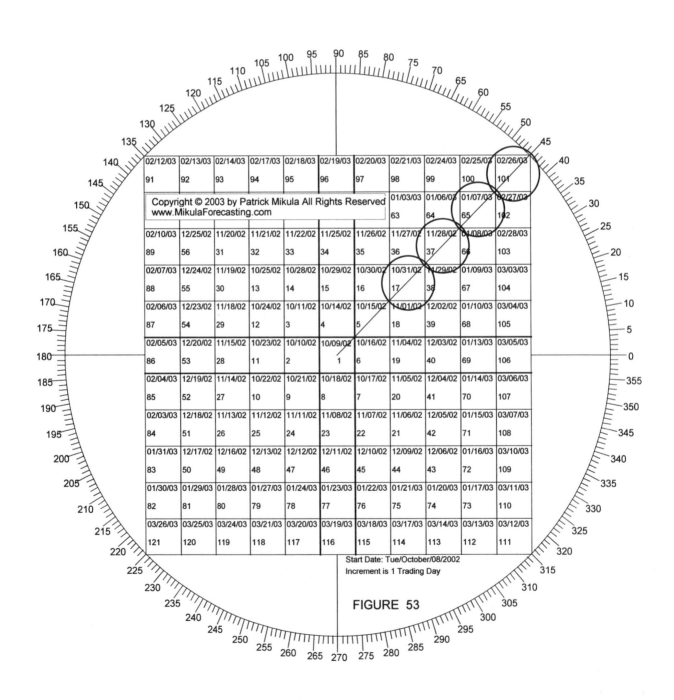

FIGURE 53

The Square of Nine in Figure 54 also accompanies the Figure 52 ALTR chart. The starting date is again Tue/October/08/2002 but this Square of Nine advances by 1 <u>calender day</u>. Figure 52 shows the calender days count using the cell numbers from the Square of Nine 45° angle as 17, 37, 65, 101 and 145. These cells are circled on the 45° angle below. The dates are in MM/DD/YY format. On Figure 54, cell 17 represents 10/25/02. Cell 37 represents 11/14/02. Cell 65 represents 12/12/02. Cell 101 represents 01/17/03. Cell 145 represents 03/02/03.

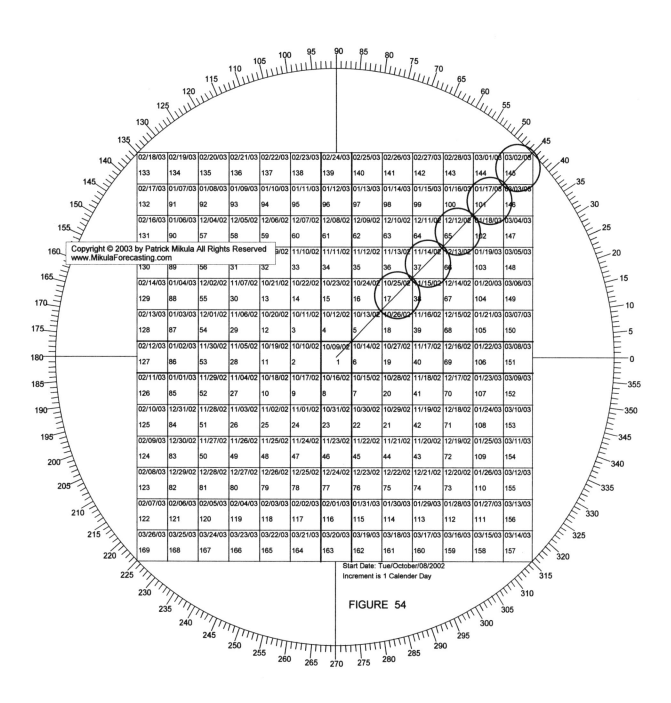

FIGURE 54

Figure 55 shows the continuation of the chart in Figure 52. The count values which correlate with a market pivot are circled. In the line diagram below the price bar chart, notice that all the market tops correlate with count values from the trading day count. All the bottoms correlate with values from the calender day count. It is a common occurrence to see the calender days correlate with all tops or all bottoms and the trading day count to correlate with the opposite.

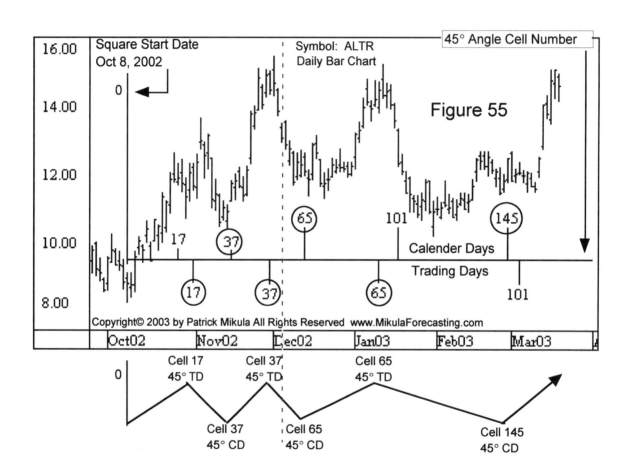

Example 3 of Forecasting Dates with Cell Numbers:
Intraday 15 Minute Honeywell, HON

Here is an intraday example of using the Square of Nine to count time increments into the future. When using intraday charts, there are three ways to count time increments. The count can be based on 24 hour time, the amount of time the market is open, or trading bars.

When making a count based on the full 24 hours in a day, the bar chart increments are divided by the total minutes in a day to find the number of time increments. This example uses a 15 minute bar chart and there are 1440 minutes in a day so there are 96 (1440/15), 15 minute increments in one day. Using a 15 minute bar chart, the count advances 96 cells on the Square of Nine each day. When counting time increments using the full 24 hours, the count includes the weekends.

The second type of time count on the Square of Nine, is to count only the time when the market is open. This is called trading session time. For example, if a market is open from 9:30 a.m. to 3:00 p.m., this is 330 minutes. Using a 15 minute bar chart, this equals 22 (330/15) time increments each trading day. In this case the count advances 22 cells on the Square of Nine each trading day.

The third way to count time on the Square of Nine, is to count only the time intervals when trading has occurred. On intraday bar charts there may be a bar interval when no trading occurred and this interval is not counted.

The strategy for using the time counting technique in this chapter on intraday charts is very different from the strategy used on the weekly and daily charts in the previous two examples. This example uses a 15 minute bar chart of Honeywell stock, HON. The starting time for the time counts is from the high pivot on May 15, 2003, 15:30 p.m. The time increment per cell on the Square of Nine is 15 minutes because a 15 minute bar chart is used.

The chart in Figure 56 shows the time counts based on 24 hour time and trading session time. Figure 56 shows all the time count values from all the diagonal cross and cardinal cross angles. When using intraday charts, the two time counts are watched for harmonization. When the 24 hour time count and trading session time count both have a value on the same bar, that bar is watched for a pivot. There are five examples of this on Figure 56. They are identified with an arrow connecting the time count and the corresponding price bar. For example on Figure 56, the 24 hour count lists a value of 553 and the trading session count lists a value of 81. These two values occur at the same time and the two counts harmonize. At this juncture, a bottom forms in the market.

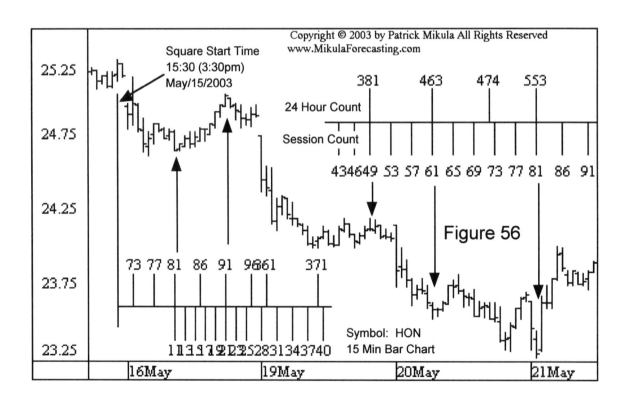

Figure 57 is a continuation of the chart in Figure 56. There is only one new harmonizing occurrence for the two time counts. This is the point at which the 24 hour count lists 757 and the trading session count lists 145. This harmonization correlates with a market top.

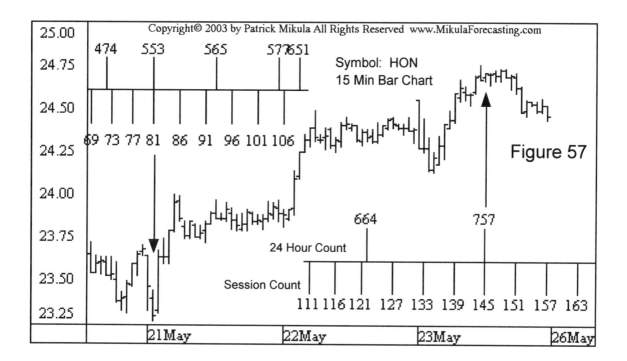

Figure 58 is included as an illustration of a Square of Nine with the time increments listed in each cell. The starting time and increment per cell are listed below the Square of Nine. Figure 58 shows the count based on trading session time.

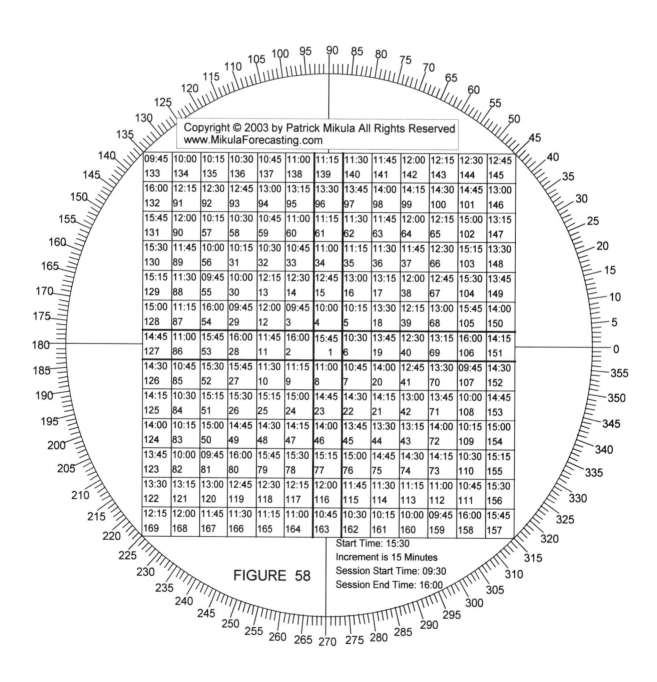

FIGURE 58

Start Time: 15:30
Increment is 15 Minutes
Session Start Time: 09:30
Session End Time: 16:00

Monthly Square

Figure 59 shows how the Square of Nine is used with monthly intervals. This Square of Nine uses a starting date of September 1929, which is the month of the stock market top before the 1929 crash. This type of chart was used by W.D.Gann with a monthly bar chart or to study long term economic cycles.

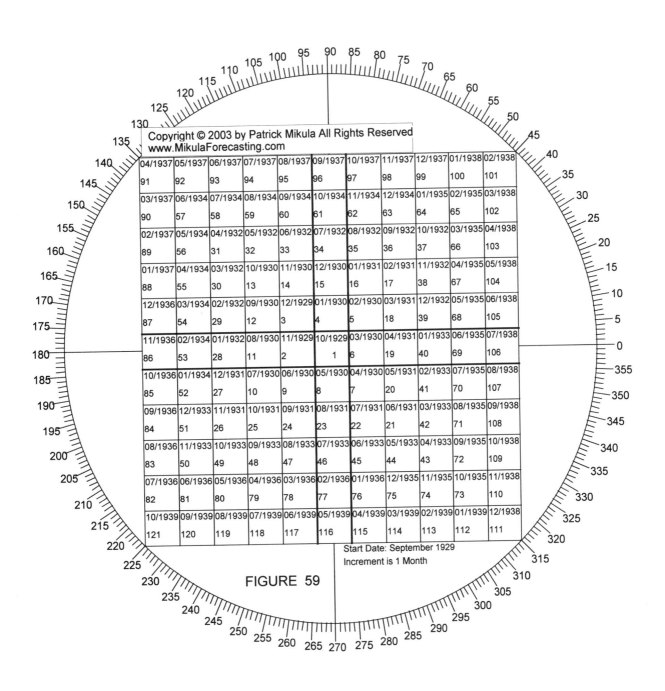

FIGURE 59
Start Date: September 1929
Increment is 1 Month

Yearly Square

The Square of Nine in Figure 60 is set to move in yearly increments. The starting date is 1776, which marks the founding of the United States of America. W.D.Gann used this type of long term yearly Square of Nine to study such things as war cycles and long term economic cycles. W.D.Gann also used the starting date of 1492 when Columbus discovered the new world for long term research of society and economics.

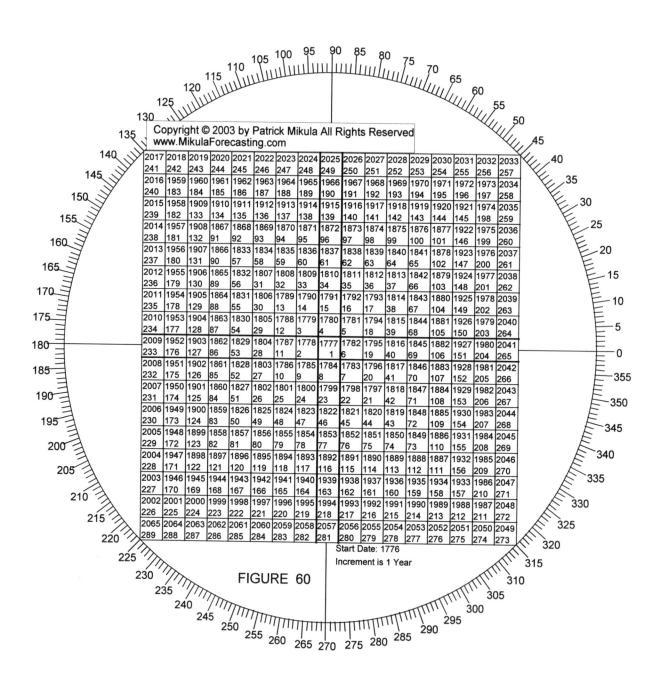

FIGURE 60

Chapter 4 Review

Objective:
Forecast pivot dates using the Square of Nine cell numbers from the cardinal cross and diagonal cross.

Step 1:
The first step is to select a top or bottom pivot date to use as the starting date.

Step 2 For Daily or Weekly Charts:
Calculate the pivot dates which fall on the Square of Nine cardinal cross and diagonal cross.

Step 2 For Intraday Charts:
Calculate the pivot times which fall on the Square of Nine cardinal cross and diagonal cross. Do this for both 24 hour time and trading session time.

Step 3 For Daily or Weekly Charts:
The third step is study the first two or three dates from each count to determine if one of the counts correlates with market pivots. If a correlation is found, the count can be used for forecasting.

Step 3 For Intraday Charts:
The third step is to identify the times which are calculated by both counts in step 2. Times which are calculated by both the 24 hour time count and trading session time count can be used to forecast intraday pivots. Watch for the two time counts to harmonize. The harmonization of the two time counts is used as a forecast for pivots.

Step 4 For Daily or Weekly Charts:
The fourth step is to use the count found in step 3 and mark the count's future dates on the chart. These future dates are pivot forecast dates.

CHAPTER 5: Forecasting Dates: Using Overlays and Two Historical Pivot Dates

This chapter shows how to forecast pivot dates using overlays and two historical starting pivot dates

Example 1 - Daily Continuous May Soybean Contract

There are two historical dates required for this forecasting method. The first starting date must be the earlier. It is used as the starting date on the Square of Nine. Figure 61 shows a continuous contract of May Soybean futures. The significant low pivot date April 24, 2001 on Figure 61 is used as the first starting date.

The second starting date is used to align the overlay's 0° angle. On Figure 61, the top pivot from July 7, 2001 is used for the second starting date.

The Square of Nine is setup so it advances the first starting date outward from the center. The 0° angle on the overlay is then aligned on the cell which holds the second start date. The dates which fall on the overlay's angles are then watched for future pivot dates.

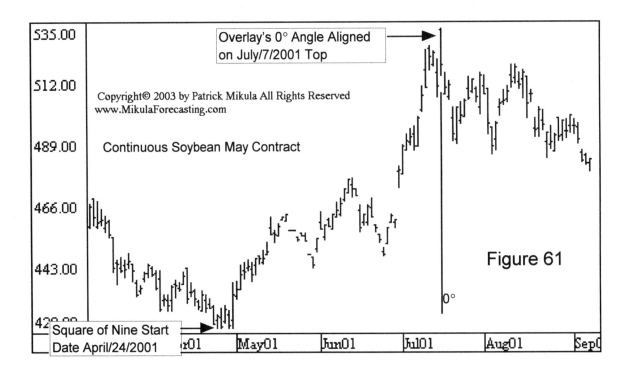

Figure 61

The current May Soybean example uses a Square of Nine with a trading day progression and a second Square of Nine with a calender day progression.

Figure 62 shows a progression based on trading days. The first starting date is April 24, 2001 and this date is written below the Square of Nine. Each cell on the Square of Nine advances one trading day. The overlay's 0° angle is aligned on the second starting date July 7, 2001, which is in cell 60. Previously in this book, it was stressed that markets tend to favor certain angles on the Square of Nine. On Figure 62 there are cells circled on the 45° angle and the 120° angle. These circled dates represent pivot dates in the Soybean market and are shown on the chart in Figure 64 and 65.

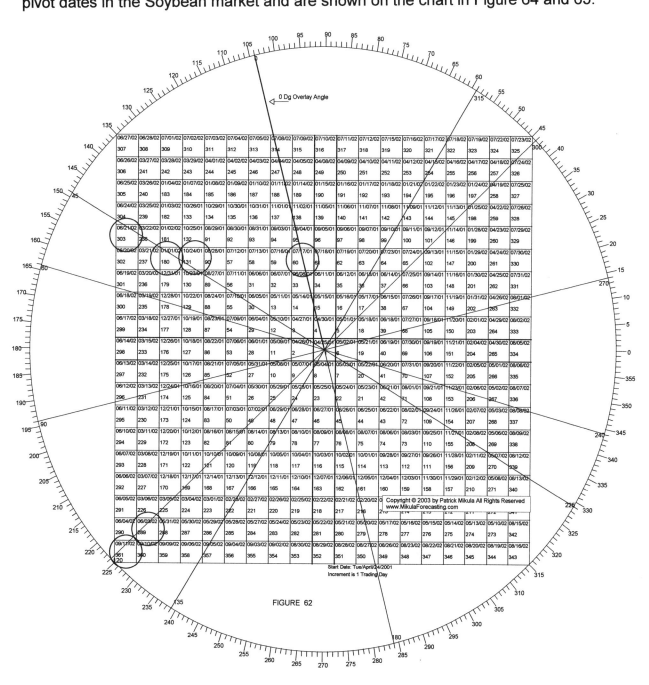

FIGURE 62

Figure 63 shows the second Square of Nine for this example. The starting date, April 24, 2001 is written below the Square of Nine. The progression is 1 calender day. The overlay's 0° angle is again aligned on the pivot date July 7, 2001, which now is in cell 84. Notice that there are a lot of circles on the 120° angle and the 45° angle. These are all pivot dates. For both the trading day progression and the calender day progression, the Soybean market favors the overlay's 45° angle and the overlay's 120° angle. These pivot dates are shown in Figure 64 and Figure 65.

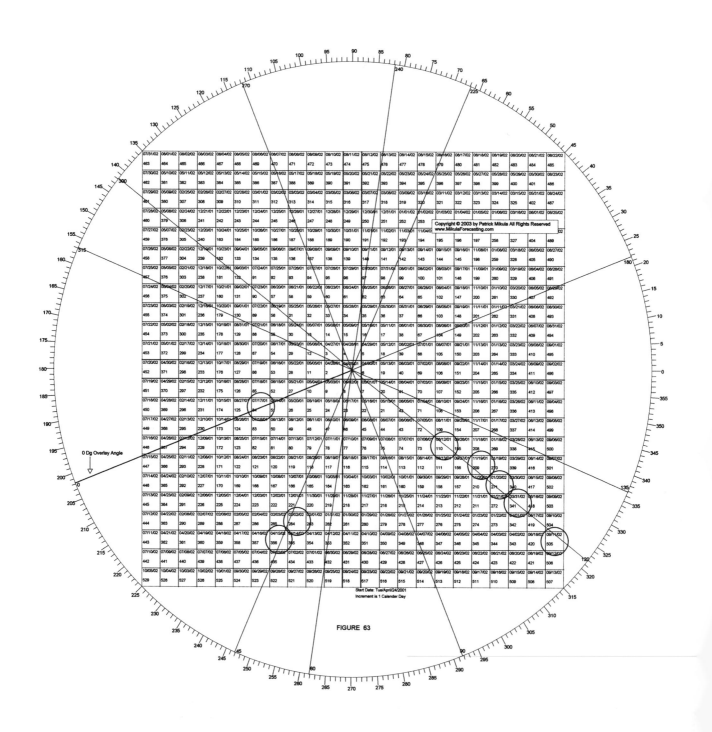

FIGURE 63

Figure 64 provides a lot of information. The overlay's 0° angle is aligned on July 7, 2001. This is represented by a vertical line below the pivot top on July 7, 2001. Starting from the July 7, 2001 top, there is a horizontal line which runs across the May Soybean chart. From this horizontal line there are upward hash marks showing the calender day count from the overlay's 45° and 120° angle. The downward hash marks represent the trading day count, again from the overlay's 45° and 120° angle. Each hash mark is accompanied by at least one number which is the cell number where the date of the hash mark is found on the Square of Nine. For the hash marks which correspond with a market pivot, Figure 64 is also labeled either 45° or 120° to indicate which overlay angle contains the date.

Below the price bar chart is a simple line diagram showing the pivots that correlate with dates on the overlay's 45° or 120° angle. All the significant pivot tops fall on the overlay's 120° angle for the calender day count. Also notice that all of the bottom pivots fall on one of the 45° angles.

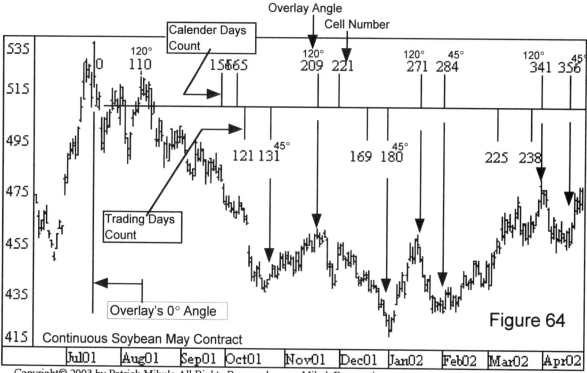

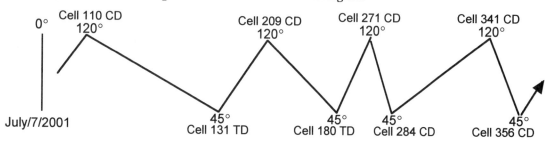

Figure 65 is a continuation of the May Soybean chart in Figure 64. The horizontal line which shows the hash marks for the Square of Nine calender day count and trading day count is moved to the bottom of the chart. The line diagram below the chart is also continued. The tops identified on this chart again form on dates from the overlay's 120° angles. The bottoms identified on this chart once more form on a date from the overlay's 45° angle.

The observation that this market favors the overlay's 45° and 120° angles can be fine tuned. The Soybean market favors the overlay's 45° angle for bottoms. The soybean market favors overlay's 120° angle for tops. Markets often favor an overlay angle for tops and favor a different overlay angle for bottoms. This is not always the case but it does happen with enough frequency to justify watching.

On Figure 65, there is a top pivot identified in September 2002. This top occurred when the dates on the overlay's 120° angle of the calender day count and trading day count harmonize. This market favors the 120° angle for tops and this top is made when the dates from both counts come together on the 120° angle.

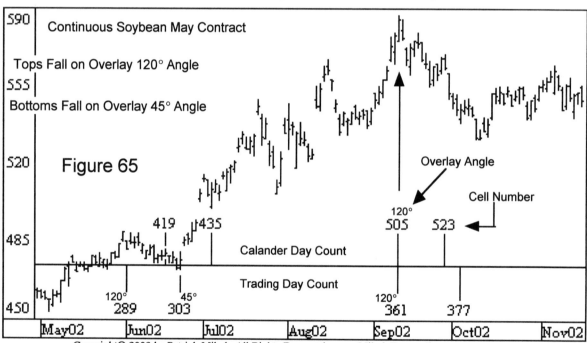

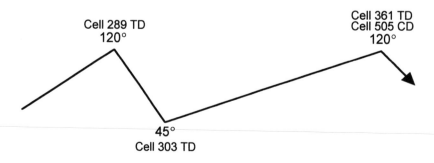

Example 2 of Forecasting Pivot Dates Using Overlays and Two Historical Pivot Dates: Weekly Wendy's, WEN

Figure 66 shows a weekly chart for the restaurant chain, Wendy's, symbol WEN. Two historical start dates are again required to apply this technique. The earlier date, July 30, 1999 is the date of a significant top in Wendy's stock and is used as the starting date for the Square of Nine. The second starting date is used to align the overlay's 0° angle. Wendy's stock made a significant bottom on March 10, 2000 and the overlay's 0° angle is aligned so it crosses over this date. See Figures 66 and 67.

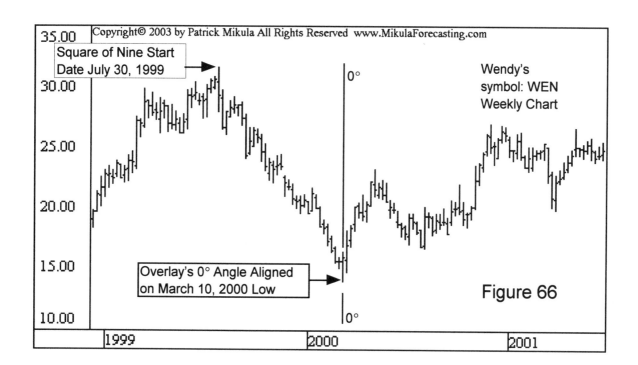

Figure 66

Figure 67 shows a Square of Nine with a starting date July 30, 1999. The Wendy's chart in Figure 66 is a weekly chart so this Square of Nine advances each cell by one week. The overlay's 0° angle is aligned on cell 32 which holds the low date of March 10, 2000. This cell is circled. Also circled are the cells along the overlays 60° and 240° angles. The tops and bottoms on the weekly Wendy's chart correlate with the dates which fall on the overlay's 60° and 240° angle. This is what is meant by a market favoring one or two of the overlay's angles. See Figure 68.

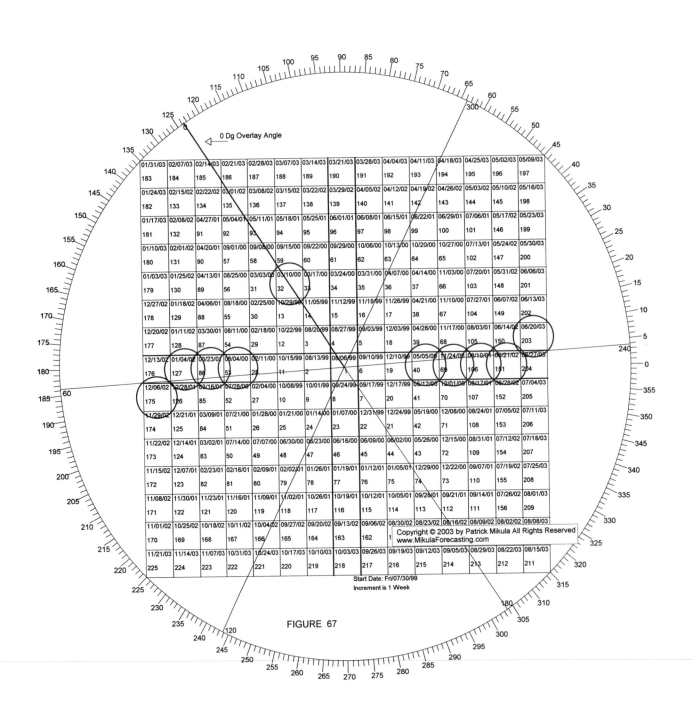

FIGURE 67

Figure 68 shows the two starting dates used with this Wendy's example. Also shown are the weekly counts from the overlay's 60° and 240° angles in Figure 67. Each weekly count value is identified by a hash mark. The count's cell number and overlay degree is shown below each hash mark. For example, cell 53 is on the 60° angle. This is on Figure 68 and Figure 67.

The line diagram below the bar chart on Figure 68, shows the sequence of dates which fall on the overlay's 60° and 240° angle. This shows the dates which fall on the overlay's 240° angle correlate with market tops. The dates which fall on the overlay's 60° angle correlate with market bottoms.

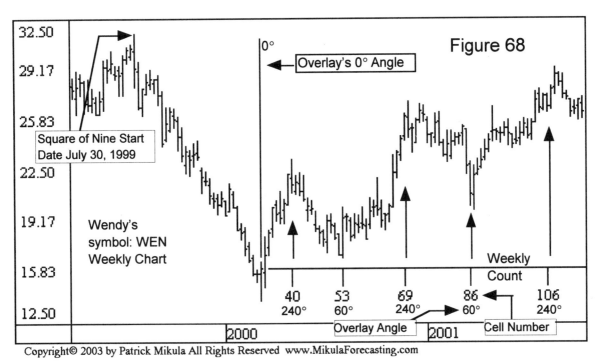

Figure 69 shows a continuation of the weekly chart for Wendy's in Figure 68. The line diagram below the bar chart continues the sequence of tops and bottoms which form between the overlay 60° angle and 240° angle.

On the bar chart in Figure 69, notice cell 127 on the overlay's 60° angle. This date should have correlated with a market bottom, but no bottom formed. This shows the pivot sequence is not flawless but is still accurate enough to be an excellent tool. Wendy's stock favored the 240° angle for market tops and favored the 60° angle for market bottoms.

Finally, the date identified by cell 151 on the overlay's 240° angle was 06/21/02. See Figures 67 and 69. Because this date falls on the 240° angle, a market top is expected around this date. On May 31, 2002 Wendy's announced the purchase of the restaurant chain, Baja Fresh Mexican Grill for $275 million. Wendy's stock then had a three week run up. On 06/21/02 Wendy's announced the completion of the acquisition and Wendy's stock made a major top very close to the date identified in cell 151 on the overlay's 240° angle.

When a sequence of tops and bottoms is established as in this example, it is common for a company to announce important news which changes the direction of the stock near the forecast pivot dates.

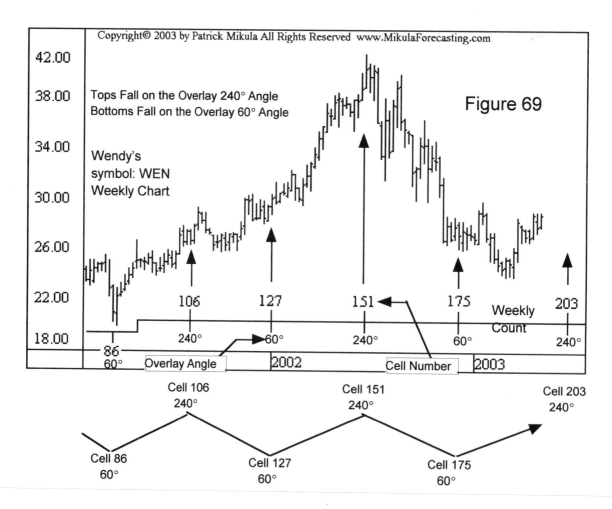

Example 3 of Forecasting Pivot Dates Using Overlays and Two Historical Pivot Dates: Daily American Express, AXP

Figure 70 shows a daily chart for American Express, symbol AXP. The first date used with this method must be the earlier and is used as the starting date on the Square of Nine. The top pivot date May/15/2002 is used as the first starting date. The second starting date is used to align the overlay's 0° angle. The next significant pivot bottom to come after the May/15/2002 top, is on July/24/2002. This low pivot date is used as the second starting date. See Figures 70 and 71.

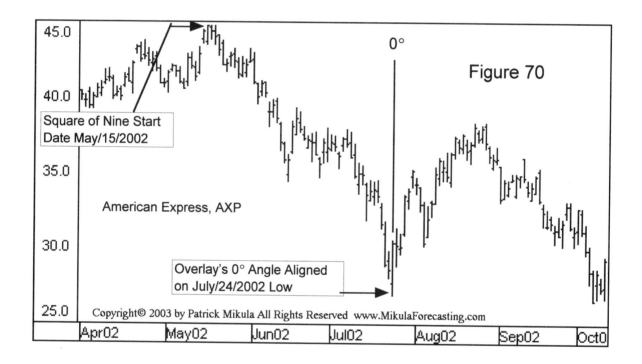

Figure 71 shows a Square of Nine which uses May/15/2002 as the starting date and has the overlay's 0° angle aligned on the date July/24/2002 which is in cell 70. The Square of Nine in Figure 71 progresses the dates using calender days. There are circled cells along the overlay's 60° angle. The cell numbers and dates along the overlay's 60° angle are as follows;

cell 101 holds 08/24/02
cell 145 holds 10/07/02
cell 197 holds 11/28/02
cell 257 holds 01/27/03
cell 325 holds 04/05/03

These circled dates represent pivot tops and bottoms in AXP.

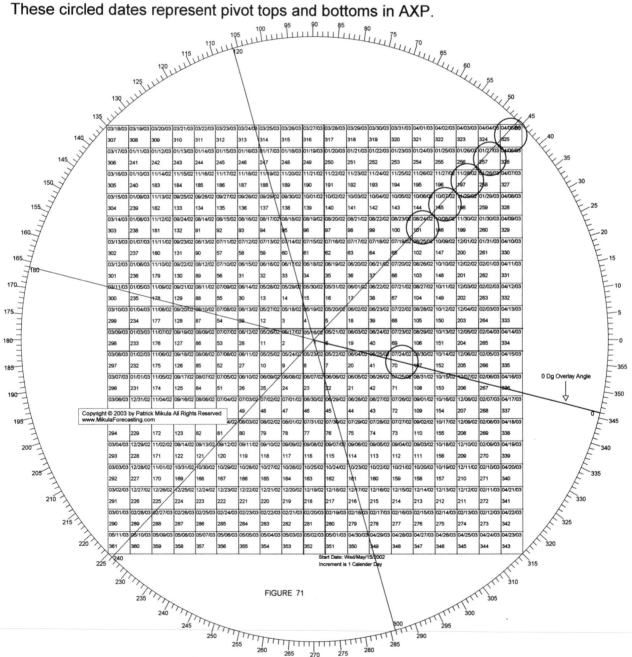

FIGURE 71

Figure 72 shows a continuation of the AXP chart. The cell and date count from the overlay's 60° angle in Figure 71, is on the chart in Figure 72. Below the bar chart, is a line diagram showing the sequence of tops and bottoms identified by the overlay's 60° angle. The date in cell 101 correlates with a pivot top. The date in cell 145 correlates with pivot bottom. The date in cell 197 correlates with another pivot top. Figure 72 shows AXP clearly favors the overlay's 60° angle for tops and bottoms.

When a market seems to favor the dates on an overlay angle, always watch for news which will trigger the expected pivot. After the dates in cells 101 and 145 correlate with pivots, the next date in the sequence from cell 197 is closely watched for a pivot. In late November 2002, very close to the date identified by cell 197, securities industry regulators announced a $350,000 fine again American Express for sales practices which did not follow proper regulatory guidelines. This negative news started the decline in AXP stock right where a pivot was expected.

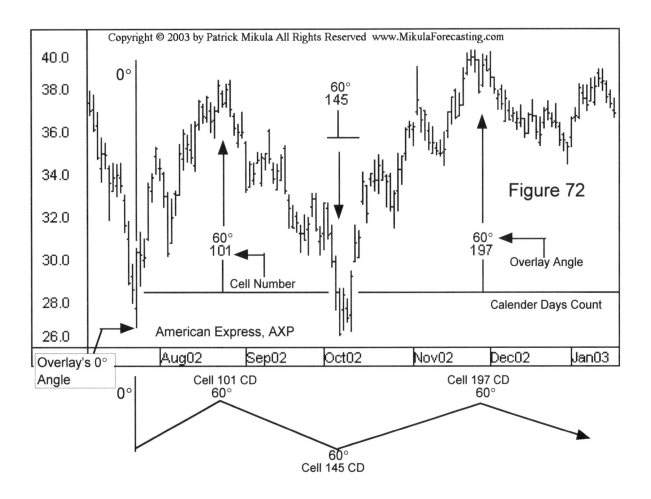

Figure 73 shows a continuation of the AXP chart in Figure 72. A sequence of pivots identified by one of the overlay angles will not continue to identify pivots indefinitely. After a period of time, the pivot sequence breaks down and no longer correlates with new pivots. On Figure 73, cell 197 correlates with a pivot top, then cell 257 correlates with a pivot bottom as expected.

When the pivot sequence reaches cell 325, a pivot top is expected. A spike top does occur at point A, but it is followed by only two declining bars. At this point, near cell 325, this sequence of tops and bottoms identified by the overlay's 60° angle seems to be breaking down. When the Square of Nine identifies a sequence of dates which correlate with market pivots, the sequence usually has four to ten accurate hits before the pivot sequence collapses.

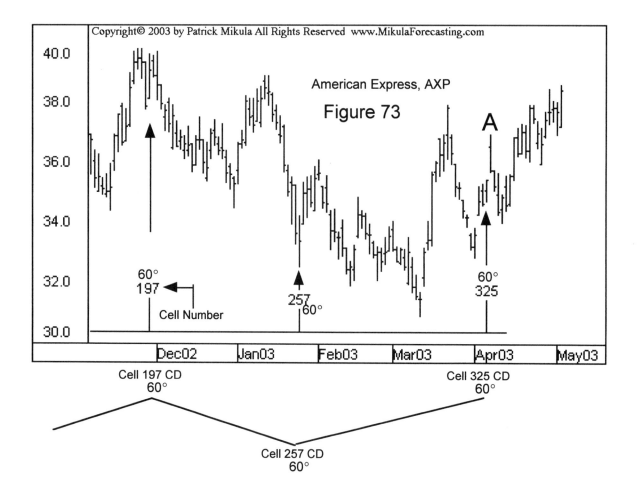

Chapter 5 Review

Objective:
Forecast pivot dates.

Step 1:
The forecasting technique in this chapter requires two starting pivot dates. The first starting date must be the earlier of the two and is used as the start date for the Square of Nine. Step 1 is to select this starting date. This step includes creating the Square of Nine with the dates listed in each cell.

Step 2:
The second starting date must come after the first start date. This second starting date is used to align the overlay's 0° angle. Step 2 is to select this second date.

Step 3:
Place the overlay's 0° angle on the second starting date found in step 2. Watch for market pivots to form on the dates which are identified by the overlay angles. If the market seems to favor the dates on one or more of the overlay angles, use the dates identified by those angles to forecast market pivots.

CHAPTER 6: Forecasting Prices: Using Progression

This chapter shows how to forecast support and resistance prices using the progression of a pivot price

Example 1 - Daily Soybean Oil

The first step to forecast support and resistance prices using the progression of a pivot price, is to select a pivot top or bottom price to use as a starting point. Figure 74 shows a chart for May 2003 Soybean Oil futures. The selected starting pivot price is the bottom pivot on October 15, 2002 at the price 19.35.

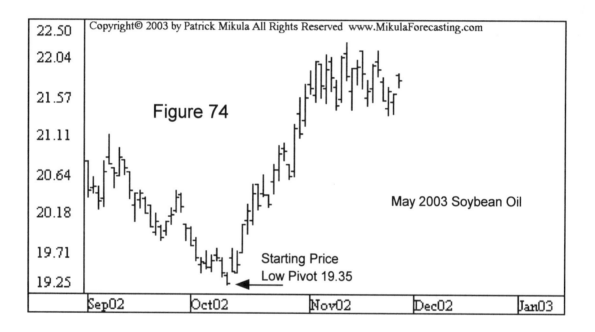

The second step is to select a price increment to advance the starting price on the Square of Nine. Each cell increases the starting price by one price increment. The price increment for this example is the minimum price movement for Soybean Oil futures which is 0.01. A frequently asked question is how to select the price increment. There is a discussion of the selection procedure at the end of this chapter.

The starting price is placed below the Square of Nine along with the price increment. The starting price and the price increment are used in a formula to calculate a new higher stock price to place in each cell. Each cell on the Square of Nine shows the standard cell number and the stock price figured with the following formula.

Formula:

Cell Number * Price Increment + Starting Price = Cell Price

For example on Figure 75, if the cell number is 81 and the increment is 0.01, and the starting price is 19.35, the price shown in cell 81 is 20.16. That is 81 * 0.01 = 8.1. The starting price is added. 8.1 + 19.35 = 20.16

W.D.Gann used the prices which fell on the cardinal cross and the diagonal cross as support and resistance levels. Each market has its own tendency and favors one or two angles from the cardinal cross and the diagonal cross.

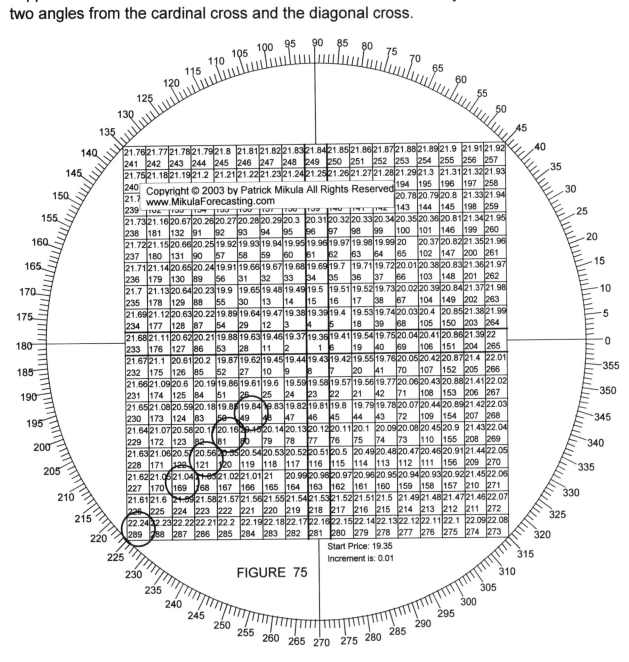

FIGURE 75

The best forecaster of the near future is the recent past. This simple idea is used to select which of the diagonal cross or cardinal cross angles to use to forecast support and resistance levels. The price values from each of the diagonal cross and cardinal cross angles are applied to the price chart. There is usually one angle which has support and resistance levels which correlate with the tops and bottoms in the market. When this angle is found, it can be used to forecast support and resistance levels.

For example, on Figure 76 the support and resistance levels from the Square of Nine 225° angle are drawn on the chart below. This is the downward left angle in the diagonal cross. The horizontal lines running across the chart are the support and resistance lines based on the prices from the Square of Nine 225° angle. On the left end of the support and resistance lines are the cell numbers from Figure 75, in which the support and resistance prices are found. The number on the right end of each support and resistance line is the price at which the line is drawn. The Soybean Oil market makes a top very close to the support and resistance price found in cell 289. This price is 22.24. This top is marked with the letter A. The top at A shows that this market favors the support and resistance levels from the Square of Nine 225° angle. The prices found on the 225° angle are drawn into the future and used to forecast support and resistance levels.

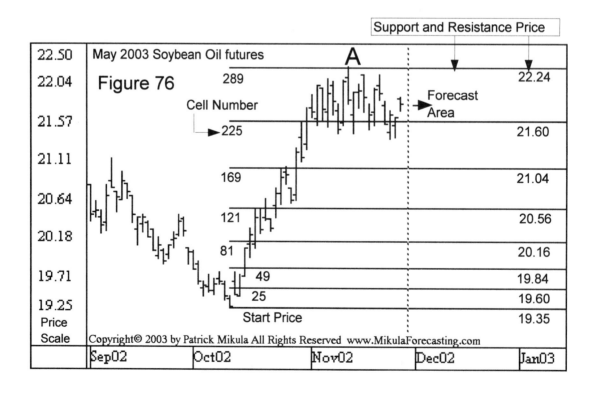

Figure 77 is a continuation of the chart in Figure 76. The letter A is the same top pivot as in Figure 76. The letters B, C, D, E, F and G, are immediately above or below a pivot which forms on a support and resistance line. This shows the Soybean Oil market continues to favor the 225° angle on the Square of Nine after point A. This is what is meant by the recent past forecasting the near future.

The Square of Nine does a good job identifying the top and bottom prices after the October 15, 2002 starting date, but it does not make the tops and bottoms occur. For example at point A, the top occurs after government reports show U.S. soybean supplies are larger than expected because of lower domestic use and lower exports. At point E, industry reports indicate export bookings are up for soybeans and the demand for soybeans and soybean oil is increasing. Even with the ability to forecast, the events in the market should be followed. Often important news is released when the prices are on a forecast support and resistance level.

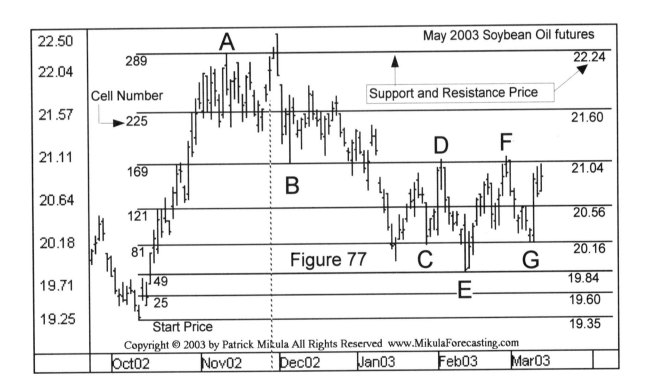

Example 2 of Forecasting Prices Using the Progression of a Pivot Price: Daily Merck, MRK

This example of forecasting support and resistance points using the progression of a price uses a Merck chart. Again, the first step is to select a top or bottom pivot to use as a starting point. Figure 78 shows a daily stock chart for Merck, symbol MRK. The July 23, 2002 low of 38.50 is used as the starting point with this example.

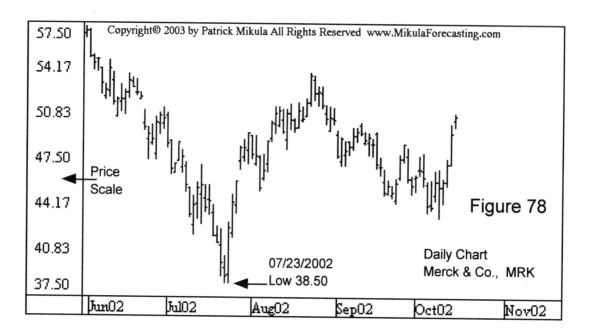

Figure 78
Daily Chart
Merck & Co., MRK

The next step is to select a price increment. On the Square of Nine, the price increment advances the starting price one increment per cell. For this example, the increment of 25 cents or 0.25 is used. A discussion of selecting the price increment is detailed at the end of this chapter. The Square of Nine in Figure 79 shows the calculation for this example. The starting price and the increment are written below the Square of Nine. The price value for each cell is then calculated and placed in the appropriate cell along with the cell number. The formula is below.

Formula:
Cell Number * Price Increment + Starting Price = Cell Price

To calculate the price for cell 86 in Figure 79, use this formula. (86 *cell number* * 0.25 *price increment*) + 38.5 *starting price* = 60 *cell price*.

Figure 79 shows the Square of Nine for this Merck example. The starting price of 38.50 and the price increment 0.25 are listed below the Square of Nine. The price in each cell increases by 0.25. The cells which hold the prices used for support and resistance levels are on the diagonal cross and cardinal cross. To determine the best angle for forecasting, compare the prices on the diagonal cross and cardinal cross to the pivot prices over the recent past. The angle with the best correlation to the pivot prices over the recent past is usually the best forecaster of the near future.

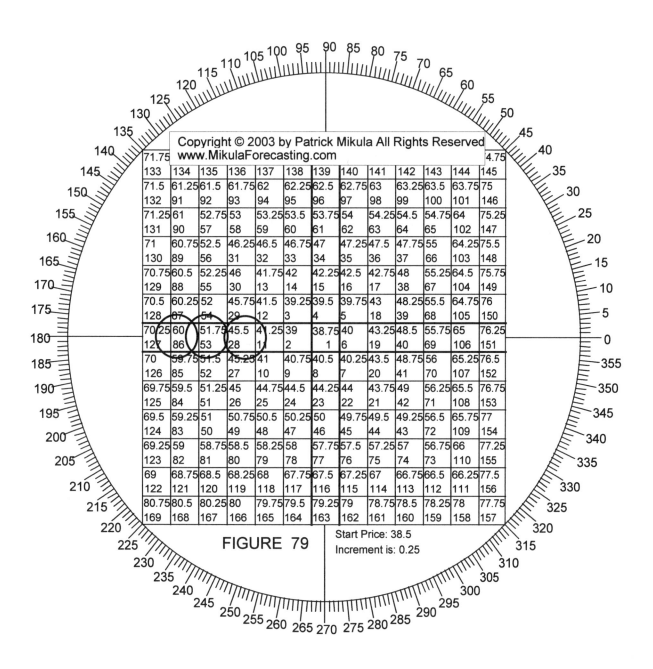

FIGURE 79
Start Price: 38.5
Increment is: 0.25

Figure 80 shows the same MRK bar chart as in Figure 78. The prices from the 180° angle on the Square of Nine in Figure 79, are drawn on the chart in Figure 80. This is the left side horizontal angle in the cardinal cross. On the left edge of each line is the Square of Nine cell number. On the right edge of each line is the price at which the line is drawn. The letters A, B and C show this market makes three pivots against these support and resistance levels. Once it is determined the market is favors the 180° angle, the price levels from the Square of Nine's 180° angle are used to forecast support and resistance levels in this market.

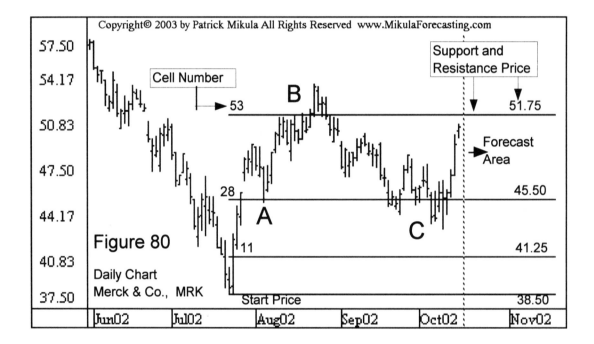

Figure 81 is a continuation of the Merck chart in Figure 80. After the pivots A, B and C occur, the market continues to form the pivots at points D, E and F. Pivots A, B and C in the recent past are able to forecast the pivots D, E and F in the near future. This procedure can be repeated in any market to forecast support and resistance prices.

The Square of Nine is able to forecast the top and bottom price levels in Merck but it does not make the tops and bottoms happen. For example, points E and F both show Merck making a top against the Square of Nine resistance level 60.00. Merck is the second largest pharmaceutical company in the U.S. and researches drugs to treat disease. At point E, the top is reached after Merck's chief researcher announces he is stepping down. At point F, Merck makes another top after the company announces it is going to buy an additional 49 percent stake in the Japanese Pharmaceutical company, Banyu, for 180 billion yen. The Square of Nine can provide accurate support and resistance levels in advance. When important news comes out about a stock while the stock price is on a support and resistance level, watch closely for a pivot.

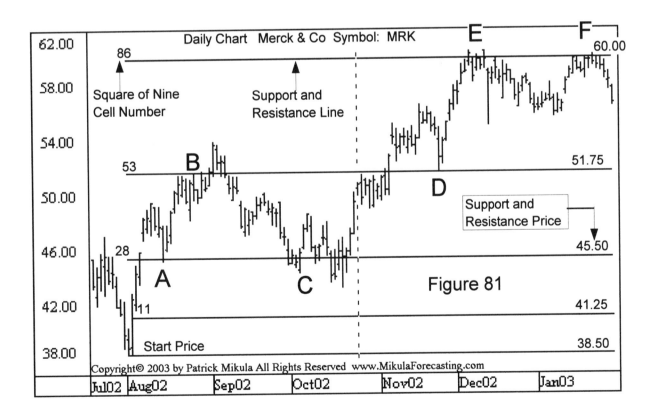

Selecting the Increment

Selecting the price increment used to forecast support and resistance levels by progressing a starting pivot price, usually generates the most questions. The price increment needs to be in proportion to the chart price scale. For example, if you are watching a stock with a 2 dollar price, you can not use an increment of 1 dollar because all the support and resistance levels will be far above the stock price.

On an intraday chart, the price scale usually covers a small range and a small increment is needed. On a weekly chart a much larger price range is covered and a larger increment is needed. The idea is to select a price increment which produces enough support and resistance levels for trading but not so many that the chart becomes crowded. The rule of thumb for selecting a price increment is that round price increments tend to work the best. A few attempts using the guidelines below should produce a good price increment for the stock or future contract you are using.

For low price stocks, start with 0.01, 0.05 or 0.10.

For medium price stocks, start with 0.10, 0.25 or 0.50.

For high price stocks, start with 0.25, 0.50 or 1.00.

For stock indexes, start with 1, 5, 10 or 25.

For future contracts, start with the minimum tick. For example with Soybean Oil, this is 0.01. For Soybeans, Wheat, and Corn, the minimum tick is 0.25. For Eurodollars, it is 0.005. The minimum tick values for most future contracts are listed in Appendix 1 at the end of this book. If you need the minimum tick for a future contract not found in Appendix 1, the futures exchange web sites have a listing of all minimum tick values for the future contracts they trade. Use multiples of the minimum tick until an increment is found which allows a reasonable amount of support and resistance levels on the chart.

Chapter 6 Review

Objective:
Forecast support and resistance levels by progressing a starting pivot price.

Step 1:
Select a top or bottom pivot to use as a starting point. Both examples shown for this technique used pivot bottoms but either tops or bottoms can be used.

Step 2:
Select a price increment to advance the starting price on the Square of Nine. See the discussion, Selecting the Increment, on the previous page.

Step 3:
Calculate the support and resistance levels which go into each cell on the Square of Nine. Use the formula seen below.

Formula:
Cell Number * Price Increment + Starting Price = Cell Price

Step 4:
Conduct a simple review of the support and resistance levels in relation to the recent market pivots. Identify the Square of Nine cardinal cross or diagonal cross angle which seems to correlate with the most pivots. Draw the support and resistance levels from the identified Square of Nine angle into the future.

CHAPTER 7: Forecasting Prices: Using Progression and Overlays

This chapter shows how to forecast support and resistance price levels using the progression of a low pivot price and overlays

Example 1 - Daily Procter & Gamble, PG

This first example uses a daily chart for Procter & Gamble. The method in this chapter uses two starting prices. The first step to forecast support and resistance prices using the progression of a pivot price, is to select a historical low starting price. This low price is used as the starting price for the Square of Nine. This price must be the lower of the two prices used with this method. For this example, the low price of 52.75 from March 10, 2000 is used. This is the lowest price in the last several years for Procter & Gamble.

The second step is to select a price on which the overlay's 0° angle is aligned. For this example, the overlay's 0° angle is aligned to the low price of 74.08 on July 19, 2002. This is shown in Figure 82. The price on which the overlay's 0° angle is aligned must be higher than the price used as the starting price for the Square of Nine.

The third step is to select a price increment to progress the starting price on the Square of Nine. For the price scale on the Procter & Gamble chart which is 70 to 95, a price increment of 25 cents per cell is appropriate.

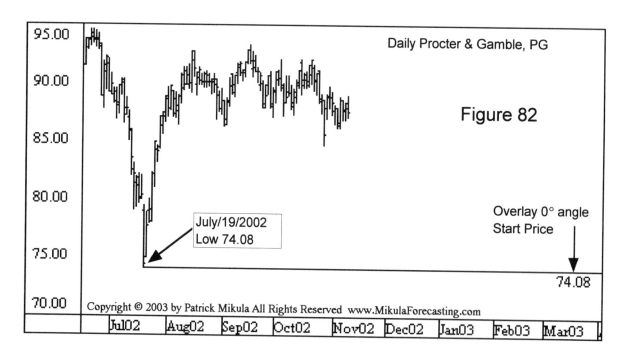

The next step is to take the prices identified by the overlay angles on the Square of Nine and draw them on the price chart. The objective in this step is to find the overlay angle which correlates with one or two pivots. Once an overlay angle is identified, the prices along this overlay angle are then used to forecast support and resistance levels.

Figure 83 shows the Procter & Gamble chart with the prices from the overlay's 120° angle drawn as support and resistance lines. On Figure 83, the letters A, B and C mark the place where the stock price forms tops against the overlay's 120° angle. The tops that form at letters A, B and C show this market favors the 120° angle and the prices from this angle are used to make forecasts.

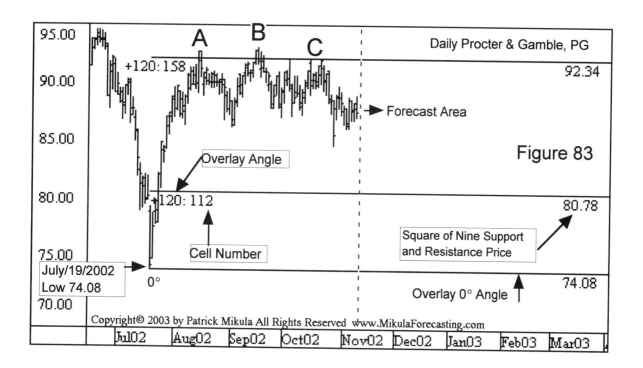

The Square of Nine in Figure 84 shows the calculation for this example. The starting price, 52.75, and the increment, 0.25, are written below the Square of Nine. Each cell on the Square of Nine advances the starting price by 0.25. Cell 1 contains the price of 60. Cell 2 shows 60.25. Cell 3 contains 60.50 and so on.

The overlay's 0° angle is aligned on the low price of 74.08 which is in cell 85. There is a circle around cell 85 on Figure 84. In cell 85 the price of 74 is located in the <u>exact center</u> of the cell. The price, 74.08, is slightly beyond the center of the cell. The overlay's 0° angle on Figure 84 is aligned exactly on 74.08.

The overlay's 120° angle also has two circles on it. The circles mark the two support and resistance levels on Figure 83.

Cell 158 has a circle around it and incorporates the price, 92.25. The exact price over which the 120° angle crosses is 92.34. This is drawn on the chart in Figure 83.

Cell 112 holds the price 80.75. The exact price the 120° angle crosses over is 80.78. This is also on the chart in Figure 83. When using this method, W.D.Gann usually rounded prices and used the price found in the cell.

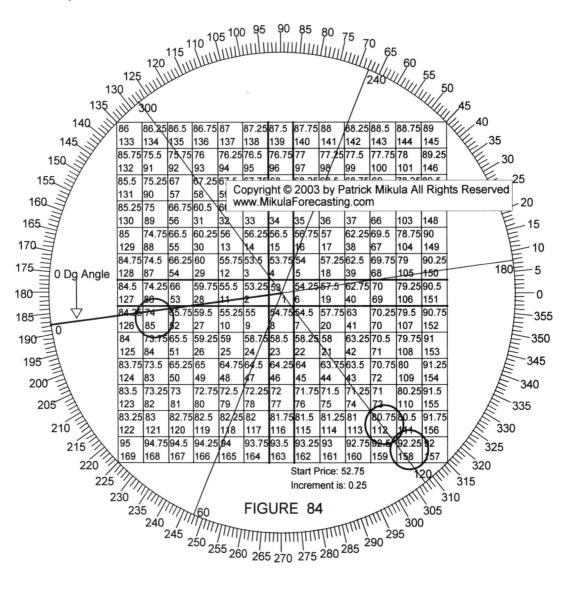

FIGURE 84

Figure 85 shows that after the top at point C, the price of Procter & Gamble falls to the forecast support and resistance line and then makes a bottom. This bottom pivot is marked with the letter D.

The Square of Nine can accurately forecast support and resistance levels but it is important to watch the news on a stock to understand why it is moving. For example, Procter & Gamble falls to the forecast support and resistance line at point D and holds there for seven bars. During that time, it is made public that Procter & Gamble is about to make a 5 billion Euro bid to buy the German hair care company, Wella. This news starts Procter & Gamble on a strong run up from the Square of Nine support and resistance level.

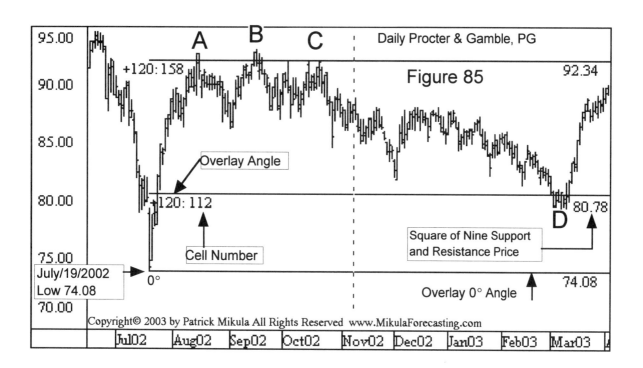

Example 2 of Forecasting Prices Using Price Progression and Overlays:
15 Minute Procter & Gamble, PG

This is another example using Procter & Gamble but this example uses a 15 minute chart. The first step in forecasting prices using price progression and overlays is to select a starting price for the Square of Nine. This is a historical low price that is lower than any of the current price data. The starting price for the Square of Nine is the low price of 74.08 from July 19, 2002

The second step is to select a price on which to align the overlay's 0° angle. Figure 86 shows the overlay's starting price at the low price 88.37 from May 1, 2002 at 10:15 a.m.. The overlay's starting price must be higher than the starting price for the Square of Nine.

The third step is to select the price increment for the Square of Nine. The price increment advances the prices on the Square of Nine one increment per cell. An increment which works well for intraday stock charts is one cent or 0.01. This increment of 0.01 is used in this example.

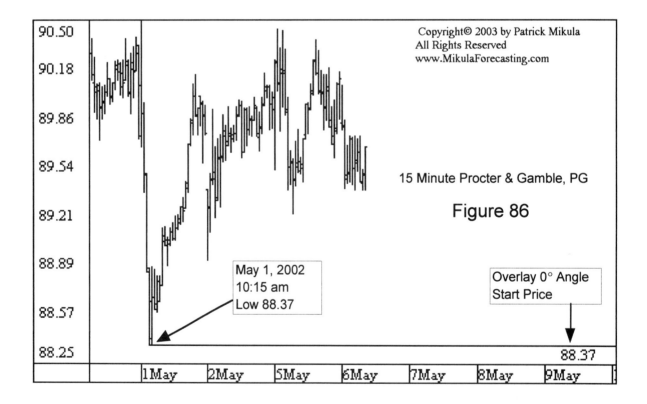

After the Square of Nine is created and the overlay is aligned on the square, the prices which fall on the overlay angles are identified. The next step is to draw the prices found on the overlay angles onto the price chart as support and resistance levels. This is done so any correlation between the chart pivots and the support and resistance prices can be found. This is how to determine which overlay angle the market favors. The angles which the market favors are used to make forecasts. On Figure 87, the prices from the overlay's 270° angle are drawn. The letters A and B mark the position where the stock makes two pivots on one of the support and resistance levels. This shows the market on this time frame favors the overlay's 270° angle.

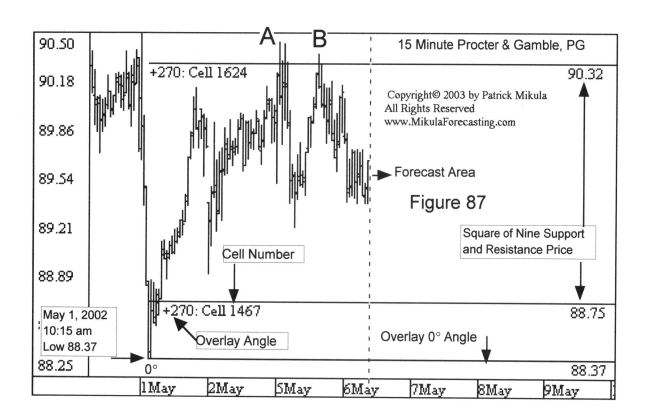

Figure 87

The Square of Nine for this example is too large to fit on one page. Figure 88 shows a section of the left side of the Square of Nine. The starting price is 74.08 and the price increment per cell is 0.01. The overlay's 0° angle is aligned on price 88.37 in cell 1429 which is not shown on Figure 88. There are circles around cells 1467 and 1624. These two cells are on the overlay's 270° angle. The price in cell 1467 is 88.75 and cell 1624 holds the price of 90.32. These cell numbers and prices are on Figure 87 where they are drawn as support and resistance lines.

Figure 88

79.01	79.94	80.95	82.04	83.21	84.46	85.79	87.2	88.69	90.26	91.91
493	586	687	796	913	1038	1171	1312	1461	1618	1783
79.02	79.95	80.96	82.05	83.22	84.47	85.8	87.21	88.7	90.27	91.92
494	587	688	797	914	1039	1172	1313	1462	1619	1784
79.03	79.96	80.97	82.06	83.23	84.48	85.81	87.22	88.71	90.28	91.93
495	588	689	798	915	1040	1173	1314	1463	1620	1785
79.04	79.97	80.98	82.07	83.24	84.49	85.82	87.23	88.72	90.29	91.94
496	589	690	799	916	1041	1174	1315	1464	1621	1786
79.05	79.98	80.99	82.08	83.25	84.5	85.83	87.24	88.73	90.3	91.95
497	590	691	800	917	1042	1175	1316	1465	1622	1787
79.06	79.99	81	82.09	83.26	84.51	85.84	87.25	88.74	90.31	91.96
498	591	692	801	918	1043	1176	1317	1466	1623	1788
79.07	80	81.01	82.1	83.27	84.52	85.85	87.26	88.75	90.32	91.97
499	592	693	802	919	1044	1177	1318	1467	1624	1789
79.08	80.01	81.02	82.11	83.28	84.53	85.86	87.27	88.76	90.33	91.98
500	593	694	803	920	1045	1178	1319	1468	1625	1790
79.09	80.02	81.03	82.12	83.29	84.54	85.87	87.28	88.77	90.34	91.99
501	594	695	804	921	1046	1179	1320	1469	1626	1791
79.1	80.03	81.04	82.13	83.3	84.55	85.88	87.29	88.78	90.35	92
502	595	696	805	922	1047	1180	1321	1470	1627	1792
79.11	80.04	81.05	82.14	83.31	84.56	85.89	87.3	88.79	90.36	92.01
503	596	697	806	923	1048	1181	1322	1471	1628	1793

— 0°

Overlay Angle 270°

Starting Price: 74.08
Price Increment 0.01

After the top at point B on Figure 89, the price of Procter & Gamble falls to point C and the market makes a bottom. The bottom pivot at point C forms precisely on the overlay's 270° angle support and resistance price. Because Procter & Gamble shows that it favors the prices on the overlay's 270° angle at pivots A and B, forecasting the next important support and resistance level is simple.

This second forecasting example uses Procter & Gamble the same as the first example. Look back to Figure 85 in the first example, and notice that the basic pattern is the same. The overlay's 0° angle is aligned on a low pivot; the overlay angles which the market favors are identified using pivot tops and finally the favored overlay angle is able to forecast the price level of the next low pivot. The important point is that Figure 85 shows a daily chart and Figure 89 shows a 15 minute chart. The same method can be applied and used for almost any time frame. The only difference is in selecting the two starting prices and selecting the price increment.

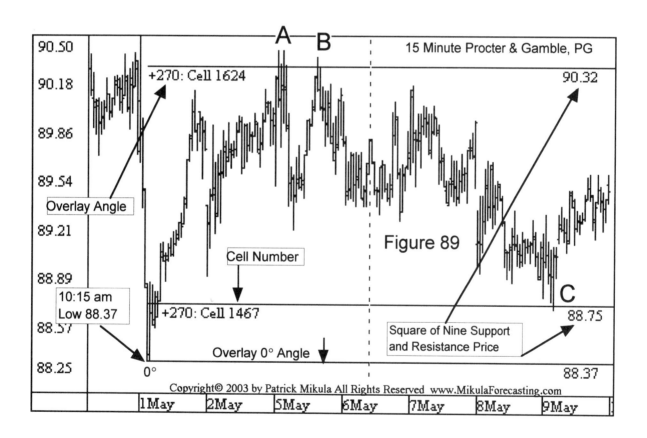

Example 3 of Forecasting Prices Using Price Progression and Overlays: Weekly Cendant, CD

Here is a weekly example of forecasting support and resistance price levels using the progression of a pivot price and overlays. Figure 90 shows a weekly chart for Cendant Corp., CD, a provider of real estate and travel services. The first step is to select a historical low price which is lower than any of the current data. This first starting price is used as the starting price on the Square of Nine. For this example, the long term low price of 6.50 from October 19, 1998 is selected.

The second step is to select the price on which to align the overlay's 0° angle. The price selected for this is the top price of 20.00 from January 4, 2002.

The third step is to select a price increment to advance the prices on the Square of Nine per cell. Based on the price range of this chart running from 10 to 22, the price increment selected for this example is 0.25 or 25 cents.

Figure 90 shows the weekly chart for Cendant with a horizontal line drawn from the top at 20.00. This horizontal line represents the overlay's 0° angle.

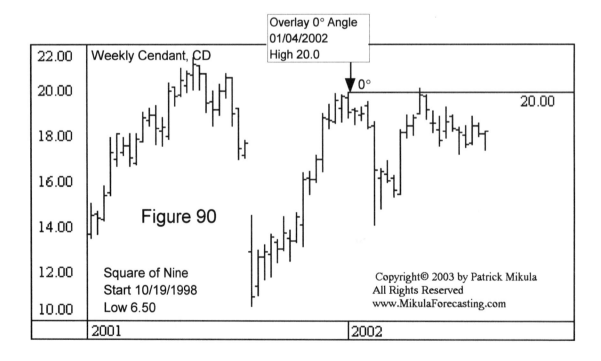

The next step is to determine if this market favors any overlay angles. This is done by identifying the prices which fall on the overlay angles and drawing them on the chart as support and resistance levels. On Figure 91, a price from the overlay's 315° angle is drawn on the chart. The letter A marks the position where the price falls and makes a bottom pivot on the overlay's 315° angle. The pivot at point A shows this market favors the prices on the overlay's 315° angle so this angle is used to forecast support and resistance prices.

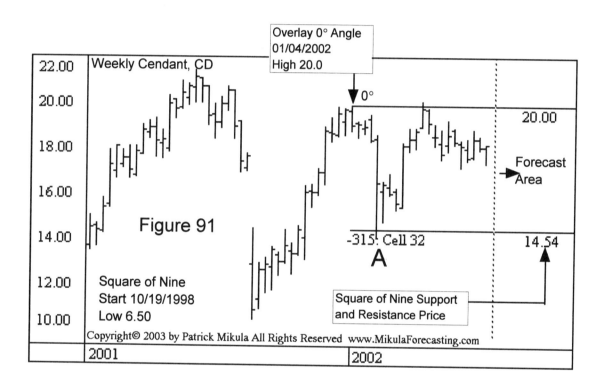

Figure 92 shows the Square of Nine for this example. The starting price is 6.50 and the price increment is 0.25. These are listed below the square. There is a circle around cell 54 which holds the price 20. The overlay's 0° angle is aligned on the price 20. There are two other circles around cells on the 315° angle. These are cell 14, which holds the price 10, and cell 32, which holds the price of 14.50. The exact prices that the overlay's 315° angle crosses are 9.94 and 14.54. These prices are on the chart in Figure 93 as support and resistance lines.

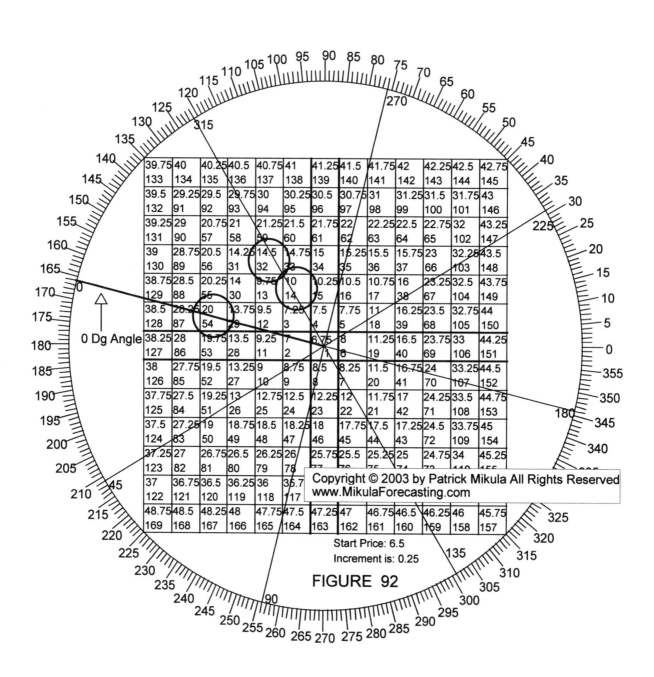

FIGURE 92

Figure 93 shows the prices from the overlay's 315° angle as support and resistance lines on the weekly Cendant chart. The market shows it favors the overlay's 315° angle at point A. Therefore, it is simple to forecast the next lower support level where the market makes a bottom pivot at point B. When the market touches the support price found on the overlay's 315° angle it makes the bottom pivot at B.

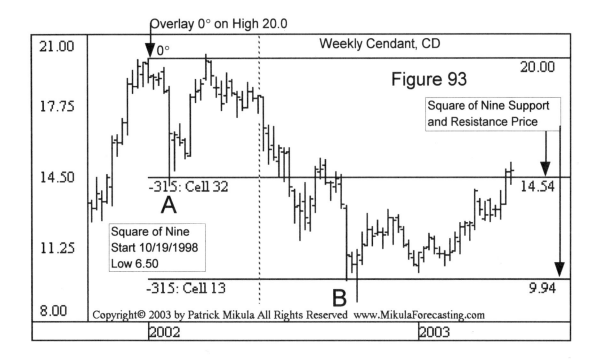

Chapter 7 Review

Objective:
Forecast support and resistance levels by using an overlay on a Square of Nine which shows the progression of the starting price.

Step 1:
The first step is to select a historical low price to use as the starting price on the Square of Nine. This historical price must be lower than any of the current price data. This price is often a futures all time low price or the lowest trading price over the past several years.

Step 2:
Step two is to select a price on which to align the overlay's 0° angle. This price must be higher than the price used as the starting price on the Square of Nine.

Step 3:
The third step is to select the price increment for the Square of Nine. Chapters 6 uses the same process to select a price increment. Read the section "Selecting the Increment" in Chapter 6, page 103. The price increment is used to advance the Square of Nine starting price one increment per cell.

Step 4:
The fourth step is to determine if the market currently favors any of the overlay angles. This is done by aligning the overlay's 0° angle on the price selected in step 2. Look for prices that fall on the overlay angles. Draw the overlay angles on the chart as support and resistance lines. If pivots form on an overlay angle, it is an indication the market favors that angle.

Step 5:
Use the prices identified in step 4 to forecast support and resistance levels.

CHAPTER 8: Forecasting Price: Using Regression

This chapter shows how to forecast support and resistance prices using the regression of a pivot price

Example 1 - Daily Teradyne Inc., TER

The first step to forecast support and resistance prices using the regression of a pivot price, is to select a pivot top or bottom price to use as a starting point. Figure 94 shows a stock chart for Teradyne Inc., TER. Teradyne manufactures test equipment for semiconductor, electronic and network systems manufactures. The selected starting price is the top pivot on December 2, 2002 at the price 17.58.

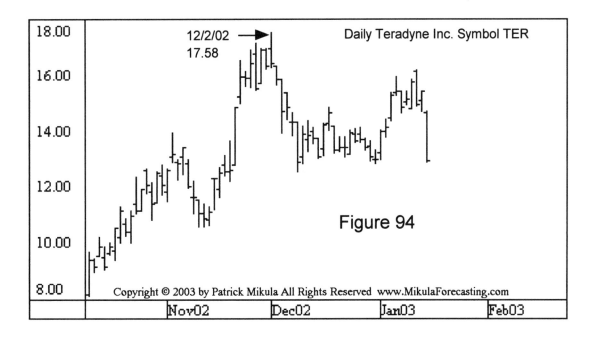

The second step is to select a price decrement to reduce the starting price on the Square of Nine. Each cell decreases the starting price by one price decrement. The price decrement for this example will be 0.05 or 5 cents. A frequently asked question is how to select the price decrement. There is a discussion of the selection procedure at the end of this chapter.

The starting price is placed below the Square of Nine along with the price decrement. The starting price and the price decrement are used in a formula to calculate a new lower stock price to place in each cell. Each cell on the Square of Nine shows the standard cell number and the stock price figured with the following formula.

Formula:

Cell Number * Price Decrement + Starting Price = Cell Price

For cell 127 this formula is:

127 *cell number* * -0.05 *decrement* + 17.58 *starting price* = 11.23 *cell price*

The Square of Nine in Figure 95 shows the Teradyne top price 17.58 used as the starting price and the price decrement is set to -0.05. This means the price values in each cell will become smaller as the Square of Nine moves out from the center. W.D.Gann used the prices which fall on the cardinal cross and diagonal cross as support and resistance price levels.

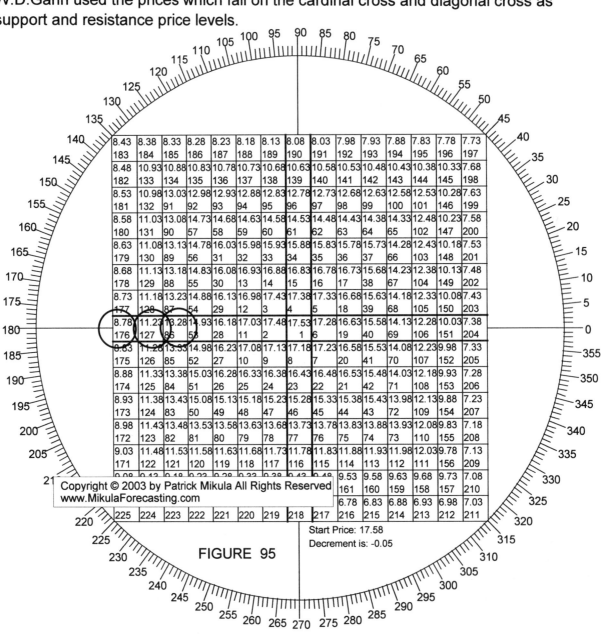

FIGURE 95

The next step is to draw the price values from the diagonal and cardinal cross angles on the price chart as horizontal price lines. After drawing the lines, determine which angle correlates with the tops and bottoms in the market. When this angle is found, it can be used to forecast support and resistance levels.

On Figure 96, the support and resistance levels from the Square of Nine 180° angle are drawn on the chart. This is the left side horizontal angle from the cardinal cross. On the left end of the support and resistance lines are the cell numbers from Figure 95, in which the support and resistance prices are found. The number on the right end of each line, is the price at which the line is drawn.

After the starting pivot top, this stock falls and makes a bottom along the support line at point A. The market then moves up and forms a top at B. Points A and B reveal that Teradyne stock favors the support and resistance levels from the Square of Nine 180° angle. The prices found on the 180° angle are drawn into the future and used to forecast support and resistance levels.

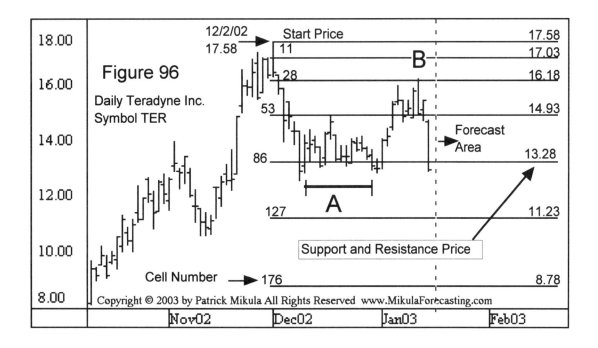

Figure 97 is a continuation of the Teradyne chart in Figure 96. After the top at point B, this market continues to form more pivots against the forecast support and resistance lines at points C, D, E, F and G. This shows the stock continues to favor the support and resistance levels from the Square of Nine 180° angle for several months after point B. The pivots at A and B represent the recent past which forecasts the pivot prices in the near future at C, D, E, F and G.

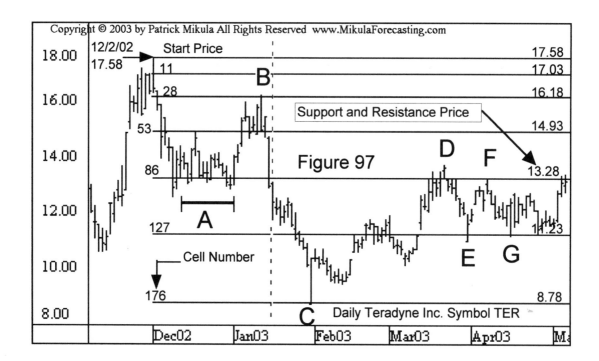

Example 2 - Weekly S&P500

This is a simple example that shows how reducing a starting price on the Square of Nine can accurately calculate a future pivot price. The initial step is to select a pivot top or bottom to use as a starting point. Figure 98 shows a weekly chart for the S&P500 cash index. The pivot selected for this example is the all time high for the S&P500 from March 24, 2000 at the price 1552.

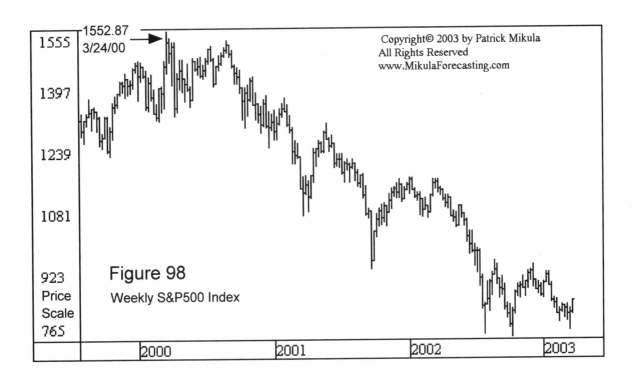

Figure 98
Weekly S&P500 Index

The second step is to select a price decrement to use in reducing the starting price on the Square of Nine. Each cell on the Square of Nine reduces the starting price by one price decrement. The price decrement for this example is negative 1. See the end of this chapter for a discussion of selecting the decrement.

The next step is to calculate the price value which is written in each cell. For example, the price written in cell 197 is 1355. To calculate this price, use this formula.

> **Formula:**
> Cell Number * Price Decrement + Starting Price = Cell Price

For cell 197 this formula is:
197 *cell number* * -1 *decrement* + 1552 *starting price* = 1355 *cell price*

Only the upper right corner of the Square of Nine for this example is in Figure 99. The next step is to select the angles from the diagonal or cardinal cross to use for support and resistance price levels. As stated previously, W.D.Gann observed that pivots gravitate toward certain angles. Those angles where pivots appeared most frequently are useful in forecasting support and resistance levels. For this example, the prices from the 45° angle are used.

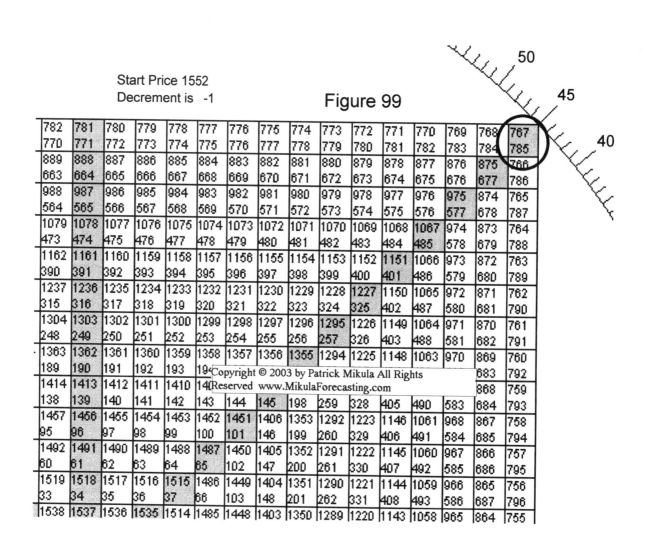

Figure 99

Start Price 1552
Decrement is -1

Figure 100 is the same weekly S&P500 chart as in Figure 98. The horizontal lines running across the chart are the support and resistance lines based on the price values from the Square of Nine 45° angle. There is a number from the Figure 99 Square of Nine at both ends of each line. On the left is the cell number and on the right is the price.

The main point of interest on Figure 100 is the letter A. This letter is below the lowest pivot on the chart which occurs in October 2002 at the price 768. This pivot occurs very close to the price identified by the Square of Nine's 45° angle, cell 785. The low price is 768 and the support and resistance level is 767. To calculate this price, the procedure is: (785 *cell number* * -1 *decrement*) + 1552 *starting price* = 767. The regression technique in this chapter calculated the bottom price value for this three year bear market in the S&P500 to within one point.

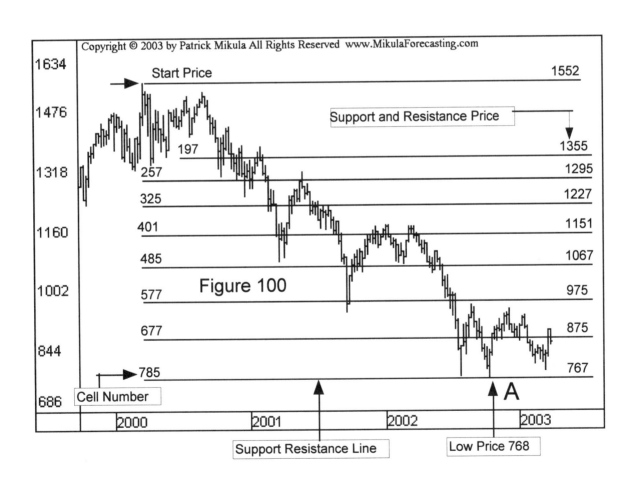

Selecting the Decrement

A price decrement has to be selected to reduce the starting price on the Square of Nine. Selecting the decrement is not an exact process so it tends to raise a lot of questions. The price decrement must be set so it has some relation to the chart's price scale. When a technique using the decrement is applied, the result should be support and resistance lines within the price range of the chart. If the decrement is too large or too small, the result will be support and resistance lines far outside the price range. The proper decrement should be easy to find using the guidelines below.

For low price stocks, start with -0.01, -0.05, -0.10.

For medium price stocks, start with -0.10, -0.25, -0.50.

For high price stocks, start with -0.25, -0.50, -1.00.

For stock indexes, start with -1, -5, -10, -25.

For future contracts start with the minimum tick. For example with Soybean Oil this is -0.01, for Soybeans, Wheat, and Corn this is -0.25. Use multiples of the minimum tick until a decrement is found which allows a reasonable amount of support and resistance levels on the chart. A simple process of experimentation is required to select a proper decrement. Appendix 1, page 203, has a list of the minimum tick values for most future contracts. If you need a tick value for a future contract not listed in Appendix 1, look up the web site for the future exchange where the contract trades. The exchange web sites list all the futures contract tick values.

Chapter 8 Review

Objective:
Forecast support and resistance levels by regressing a starting pivot price.

Step 1:
Select a top or bottom pivot to use as a starting point. Both examples in this chapter used pivot tops but either tops or bottoms can be used.

Step 2:
Select a price decrement to reduce the starting price on the Square of Nine. See, Selecting the Decrement, on the previous page.

Step 3:
Use the formula below to calculate the price for each Square of Nine cell.

> **Formula:**
> Cell Number * Price Decrement + Starting Price = Cell Price

Step 4:
Do a simple review of the support and resistance levels in relation to the recent market pivots. Identify the Square of Nine angle from the diagonal or cardinal cross which seems to correlate with the most pivots. Use this Square of Nine angle to forecast support and resistance levels on the price chart. Remember, the recent past provides the best chance to forecast the near future.

CHAPTER 9: Forecasting Prices: Using Regression and Overlays

This chapter shows how to forecast support and resistance price levels using the regression of a high pivot price and overlays

Example 1 - Daily Wheat

In this chapter, a high price is used as the starting price on the Square of Nine. The high price is regressed by a decrement. Once this Square of Nine is set up, the overlay is aligned on a price that is lower than the square starting price.

The first step is to select a high price that is higher than any of the other prices which are used with the example. For this example, the top of 459.00 from April 21, 1997 in the July 1997 Wheat contract is used. This is on the chart in Figure 101. We have selected this high price because it is a major top in the July contract. When selecting historical prices for a futures contract, it is a good idea to select historical prices from the same contract month. In this case the July contract. This high price will be the starting price for the Square of Nine.

The second step is to select the decrement which is used to regress the starting price per cell. In this example, the decrement is negative -0.25. This value is simply the minimum tick for Wheat futures. When using a futures contract, the minimum tick is the most common decrement.

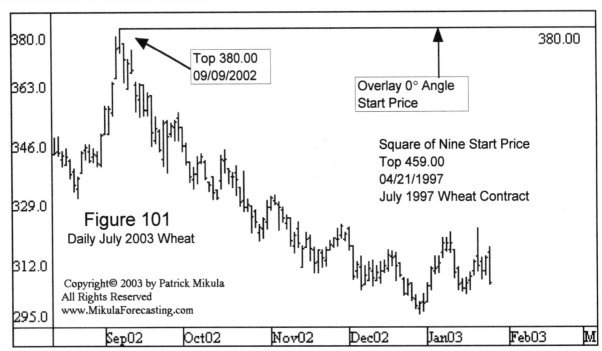

Figure 101
Daily July 2003 Wheat

The third step is to select a second pivot price on which to align the overlay's 0° angle. This pivot price must be lower than the high price selected in step one. This pivot price can be either a top or a bottom. In this example, the top price of 380.0 from Sept. 9, 2002 is used to align the overlay's 0° angle. This is on the bar chart in Figure 102.

After the Square of Nine is set up and the overlay is aligned on a pivot, the next step is to identify which overlay angles are favored by the market. The overlay angles cross over prices on the Square of Nine and these prices are used as support and resistance levels. On Figure 102, the prices that the overlay's 90° angle and the overlay's 180° angle cross over, are drawn as support and resistance levels. On Figure 102, the letters A, B, C and D mark pivots that occur near the overlays's 90° and 180° angles. This market favors these two angles in the Square of Nine. The overlays's 90° and 180° angles are used to forecast support and resistance levels.

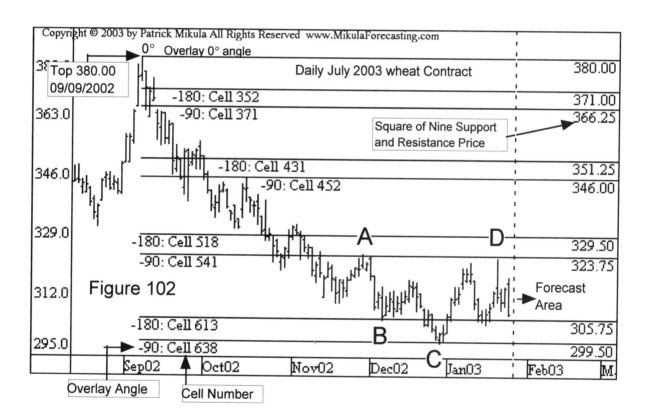

Figure 103 shows the Square of Nine for this example. The starting price of the square is 459.0 and the decrement is -0.25. This means each square is decreased by -0.25. The overlay's 0° angle is aligned on the price of 380.0 which is in cell 316. There is a circle around this cell. There is also a circle around cell 518 with the price 329.50, cell 613 with the price 305.75 and cell 716 with the price 280.0. These cells are all on the overlay's 180° angle. Also circled on Figure 103, are: cell 638 - price 299.5 and cell 541 - price 323.75. These cells are on the overlay's 90° angle. These circled cells represent the support and resistance prices where the market makes the tops and bottoms at points A, B, C, D, E, F and G on bar charts in Figure 102 and 106. The Square of Nine in Figure 103 uses small type so there are two additional pictures of this square in Figures 104 and 105.

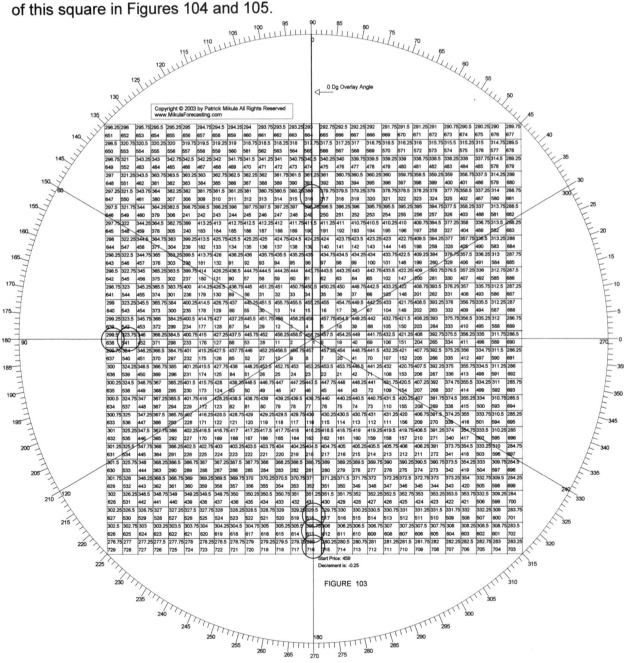

FIGURE 103

Figure 104

299.25	323.5	345.75	366	384.25	400.5	414.75	427	437.2
639	542	453	372	299	234	177	128	87
299.5	323.75	346	366.25	384.5	400.75	415	427.25	437.5
638	541	452	371	298	233	176	127	86
299.75	324	346.25	366.5	384.75	401	415.25	427.5	437.7
637	540	451	370	297	232	175	126	85
300	324.25	346.5	366.75	385	401.25	415.5	427.75	438
636	539	450	369	296	231	174	125	84
300.25	324.5	346.75	367	385.25	401.5	415.75	428	438.2
635	538	449	368	295	230	173	124	83
300.5	324.75	347	367.25	385.5	401.75	416	428.25	438.5
634	537	448	367	294	229	172	123	82
300.75	325	347.25	367.5	385.75	402	416.25	428.5	428.7

Figure 105

291	226	225	224	223	222	221	220	219	218	217	216
386.5	386.75	387	387.25	387.5	387.75	388	388.25	388.5	388.75	389	389
290	289	288	287	286	285	284	283	282	281	280	279
368.75	369	369.25	369.5	369.75	370	370.25	370.5	370.75	371	371.25	371
361	360	359	358	357	356	355	354	353	352	351	350
349	349.25	349.5	349.75	350	350.25	350.5	350.75	351	351.25	351.5	351
440	439	438	437	436	435	434	433	432	431	430	429
327.25	327.5	327.75	328	328.25	328.5	328.75	329	329.25	329.5	329.75	330
527	526	525	524	523	522	521	520	519	518	517	516
303.5	303.75	304	304.25	304.5	304.75	305	305.25	305.5	305.75	306	306
622	621	620	619	618	617	616	615	614	613	612	611
277.75	278	278.25	278.5	278.75	279	279.25	279.5	279.75	280	280.25	280
725	724	723	722	721	720	719	718	717	716	715	714

Start Price: 459
Increment is: -0

In this example the Wheat market is shown to favor the support and resistance lines from the -90° and 180° overlay angles. After the favored angles are identified, the support and resistance lines are drawn into the future. These lines work as a pivot level forecast. Figure 106 shows a continuation of the July 2003 wheat chart shown previously in Figure 102. After the overlay angle, that this market favors is identified, the market continues on to make a top at point E and two bottoms at points F and G.

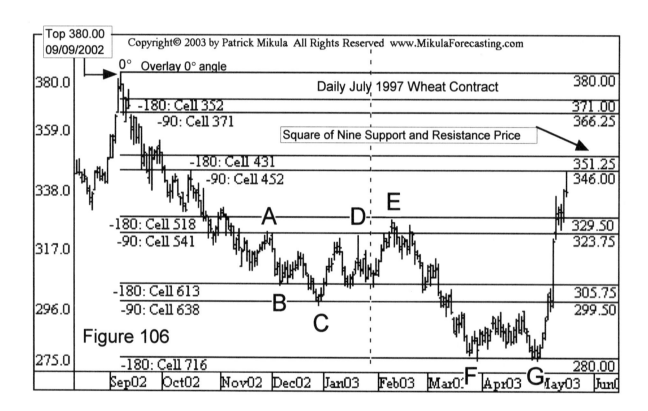

Figure 106

Example 2 of Forecasting Prices Using Price Regression and Overlays
Daily NASDAQ 100 Index

The next example uses a daily chart of the NASDAQ 100 Index. The first step is to select a high price to use as the starting price for the Square of Nine. This example uses the all time high price for the NASDAQ 100 Index. The price is 4816 from March 24, 2000. The decimal point is ignored.

The second step is to select a decrement to reduce the starting price per cell. This example uses a high price so negative -10 is used for the decrement.

The third step is to select a pivot on which to align the overlay's 0° angle. This can be a top pivot or a bottom pivot. For this example the top price of 1734 from December 6, 2001 is used to align the overlay.

Figure 107 shows the 0° angle aligned to the 1734 top on the NASDAQ 100 Index.

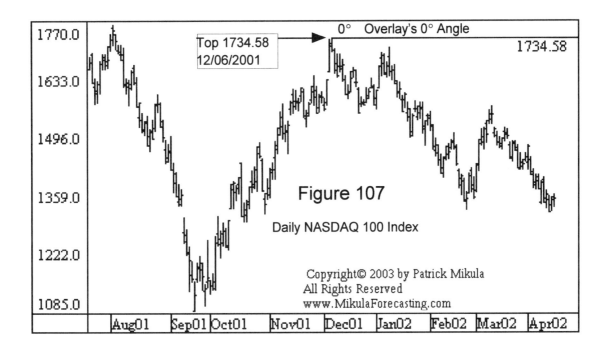

The next step is to determine if there is an overlay angle which the market favors. If an angle correlates with pivot tops or bottoms, then the market is said to favor that angle. On the bar chart in Figure 108, the letters A and B mark a bottom and top pivot near the overlay's 270° angle. This one angle has two pivots form near it. This indicates the NASDAQ 100 Index favors the overlay's 270° angle.

The next step is to draw into the future the prices located on the overlay's 270° angle. These price levels become forecast support and resistance levels. This is on the bar chart in Figure 110.

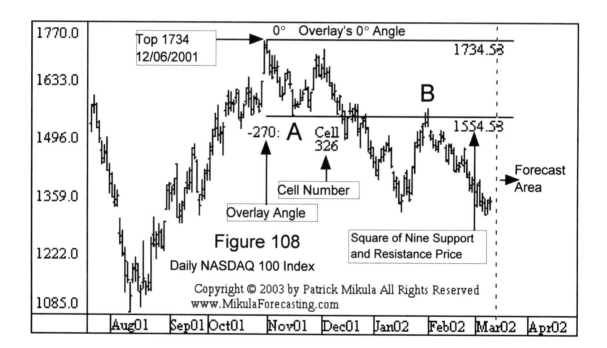

Figure 109 shows the Square of Nine for this NASDAQ 100 Index example. The Square of Nine starting price is 4816. The decrement which reduces the price in each cell is -10. The overlay's 0° angle is aligned on the top price of 1734 which is between cells 308 and 309. This starting value is circled on the square. Also circled on Figure 109, are the prices identified by the overlay's 270° angle which correlate with pivot points. This is on the bar chart in Figure 110.

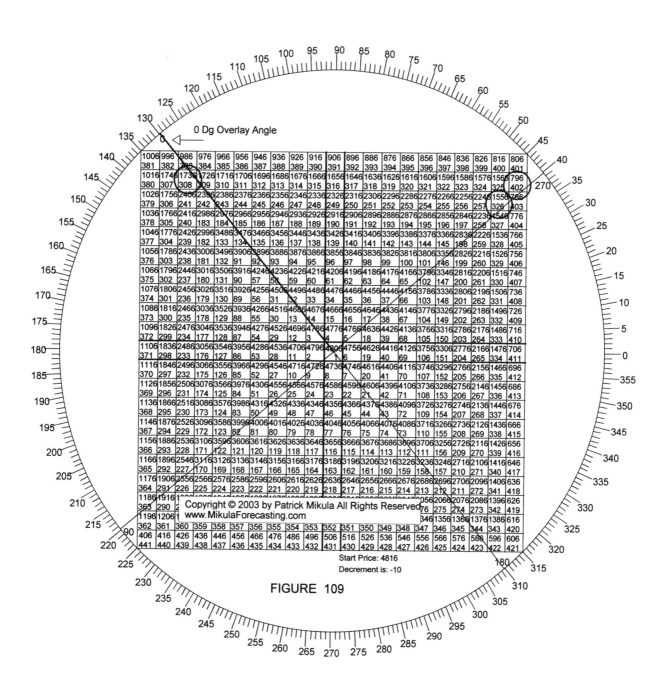

FIGURE 109

Figure 110 shows price levels from the overlay's 270° angle, drawn as support and resistance lines. After this market shows that it favors the overlay's 270° angle at points A and B, the market falls and makes a significant bottom at point C. This again shows that the overlay angles which a market favors can be used to successfully forecast price levels.

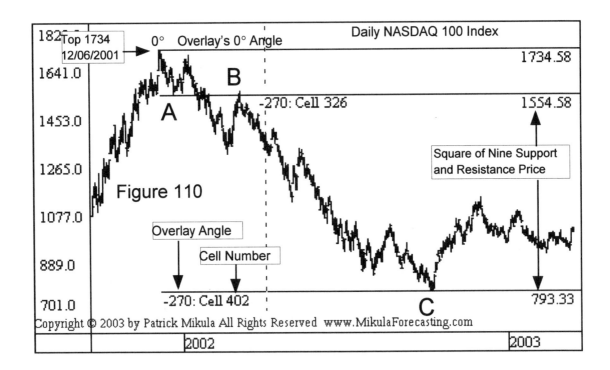

Example 3 of Forecasting Prices Using Price Regression and Overlays: Daily Corn

This is the final example for Chapter 9. This is a shorter example than the previous two with only one price chart and one Square of Nine. The first step is to select a high price to use as the starting price on the Square of Nine. For this example, the all time high for July Corn futures is used. This is the 554.50 top from July 12, 1996.

The second step is to select a decrement. The decrement is used to reduce the price per cell. In this example, the minimum tick for Corn which is 0.25, is used. The decrement is negative -0.25.

The third step is to select the pivot price on which to align the overlay's 0° angle. This can be either a pivot high or a pivot low. For this example the top price of 290.25 from September 11, 2002 is used to align the overlay.

Figure 111 shows the July 2003 Corn futures contract with the overlay's 0° angle drawn from the top at 297.25. There are two additional horizontal lines drawn on this chart. Both of these lines are drawn at prices found on the overlay's 0° angle. This means the support and resistance lines are 360° apart on the Square of Nine. After the market falls from the 9/11/2002 top, it declines two full rotations around the Square of Nine and makes two bottom pivots at points A and B.

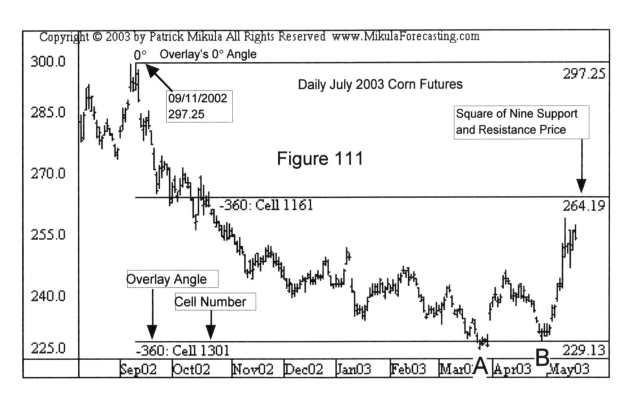

Figure 112 shows the Square of Nine for this example which is using Corn futures. The overlay's 0° angle is aligned on the price 297.25 which is in cell 1029. The two support prices which are on the same 0° angle are: 264.19 in approximately cell 1161 and 229.13 in approximately cell 1301. These cells are circled on the Square of Nine.

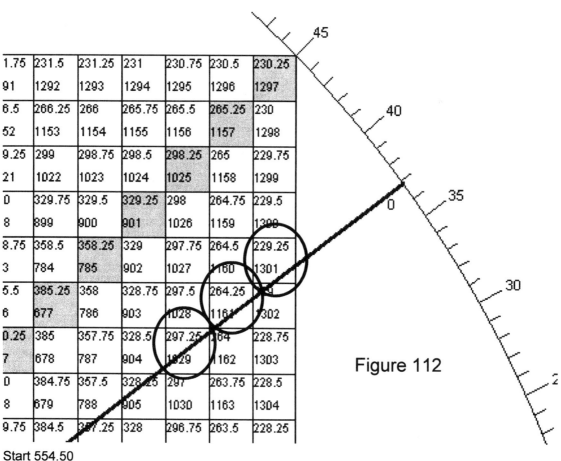

Figure 112

Start 554.50
Decrement -0.25

Chapter 9 Review

Objective
Forecast support and resistance levels using the overlay on a Square of Nine which shows a regressed starting price.

Step 1:
The first step is to select a historical high price which will be used as the starting price on the Square of Nine. This historical price must be higher than any of the current price data. This price is often a futures all time high price or the highest trading price over the past several years.

Step 2:
Step two is to select a price to align the overlay's 0° angle. This price must be lower than the price used as the starting price on the Square of Nine.

Step 3:
The third step is to select the price decrement. The process to select a decrement is the same for the methods in Chapter 8. Read the section in Chapter 8 page 125 titled, Selecting the Decrement. The price decrement is used to reduce the Square of Nine starting price one decrement per cell.

Step 4:
The fourth step is to determine if the market currently favors any of the overlay angles. This is done by aligning the overlay's 0° angle on the price selected in step 2 and then identifying the prices which fall on the overlay angles. The overlay angles are then drawn on the chart as support and resistance lines. If pivots form on an overlay angle this is an indication that the market is favoring this angle.

Step 5:
Identify the overlay angles which the market favors. Use the prices from these overlay angles to forecast support and resistance levels.

CHAPTER 10: Forecasting Price: Using a Zero Base

This chapter shows how to forecast support and resistance prices using a Square of Nine with a zero base and an increment other than one

Example 1 - Daily Minnesota Mining & Manufacturing Co., MMM

To forecast price using a zero base, this method again uses the cardinal cross and diagonal cross to locate support and resistance levels. The starting price on the Square of Nine is set to zero and the increment is set to a value other than one(1). Figure 113 shows a chart for Minnesota Mining & Manufacturing, symbol MMM. The price increment on the Square of Nine in Figure 114, is set to 0.50. Across the chart in Figure 113 are the support and resistance lines. The lines have a number at each end. On the left end is the cell number, on the right end is the price at which the line is drawn. All of the angles from the cardinal and diagonal cross are used to create the support and resistance lines on Figure 113.

To forecast support and resistance lines with this method, there must be a few pivots in the recent past that formed on the support and resistance lines. On Figure 113, the pivots at A, B and C are on the support and resistance lines. After these pivots formed on the support and resistance lines, expect a few more pivots to form against the same support and resistance lines in the near future.

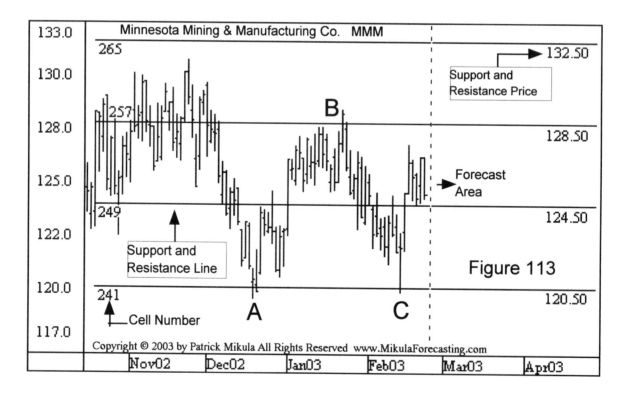

Given the price range for MMM, an appropriate increment to use is 0.25, 0.50 or 1.00. This example will use 0.50. The Square of Nine in Figure 114 is used to create the support and resistance levels on the chart in Figure 113. Calculating the price values which go into each cell requires the simple formula below. For example, the price in cell 149 is calculated by, 149 *cell number* * 0.50 *increment* = 74.50 *cell price.*

Formula:
Cell Number * Price Increment = Cell Price

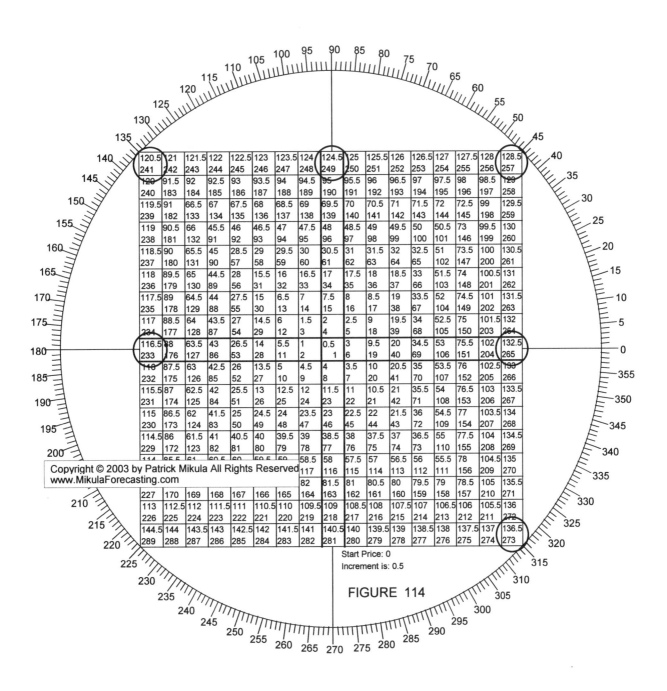

FIGURE 114

Figure 115 is a continuation of the bar chart in Figure 113. After pivots A, B and C, this market goes on to make pivots D, E and F on the forecast support and resistance lines.

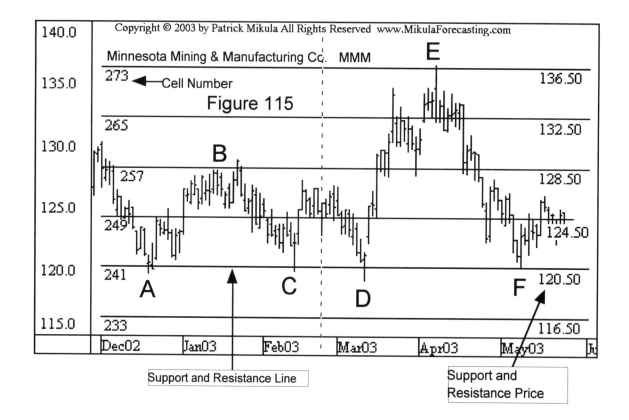

Example 2 of Forecasting Prices Using a Zero Base:
Daily Gold

The next example uses the daily Gold chart in Figure 116. This example uses a price increment of 5 on the Square of Nine. The support and resistance lines are drawn horizontally across the chart. On each line the cell number is on the left edge and the price at which the line is drawn, is on the right edge.

To make a forecast of support and resistance levels using this method, a few pivots must first form on the support and resistance lines. Only after a few historical pivots form on the support and resistance lines can the lines be used to forecast. On the chart in Figure 116, the Gold market makes a top at point A on one of the support and resistance lines. After point A, these lines can be used to forecast support and resistance.

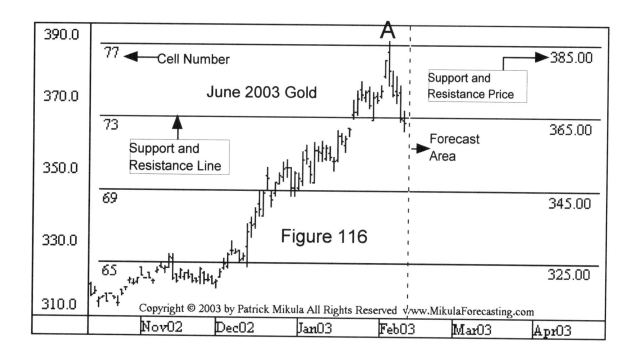

Figure 116

Figure 117 is the corresponding Square of Nine for the chart in Figure 116. The starting number on the Square of Nine is zero. The price in each cell increases by 5. The support and resistance lines drawn on Figure 116 are from all the angles in the cardinal cross and diagonal cross. To calculate the price which goes into each cell on the Square of Nine, use the formula below. The price for cell 88 is, 88 *cell number* * 5 *increment* = 440 *cell price*.

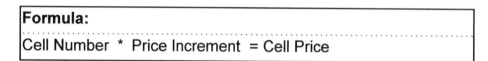

Formula:
Cell Number * Price Increment = Cell Price

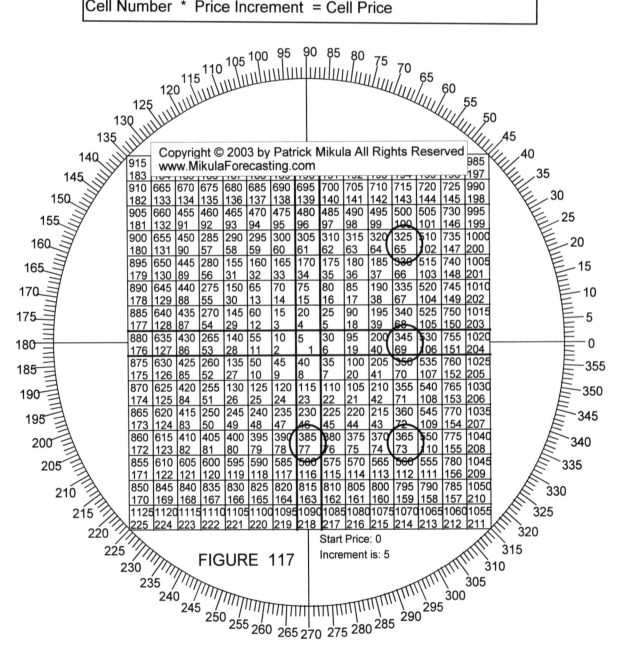

FIGURE 117

Figure 118 is a continuation of the chart in Figure 116. After the top at point A, the Gold market proceeds to make a pivot bottom at point B and C. The recent past is the best predictor of the near future. The only way to predict the support and resistance levels at points B and C is to use the success of the support and resistance levels at point A.

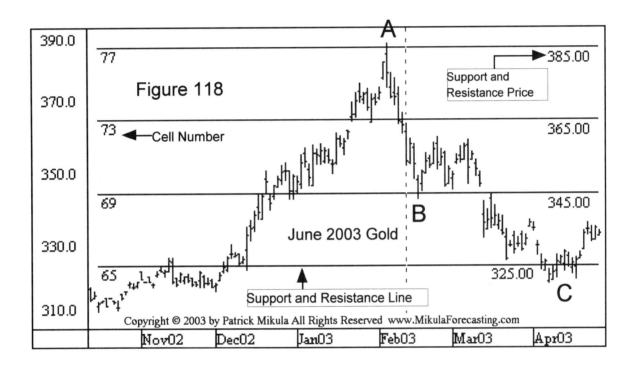

Chapter 10 Review

Objective:
Forecast support and resistance levels.

Step 1:
Set the Square of Nine starting price to zero.

Step 2:
Select a price increment which is not equal to one. This chapter uses the same process to select a price increments as is used in Chapter 6. Read the section "Selecting the Increment" in Chapter 6, page 103. The price increment is used to advance the Square of Nine starting price one increment per cell.

Step 3:
Calculate the price which goes into each Square of Nine cell by multiplying the cell number by the increment. Use the formula below.

> **Formula:**
> Cell Number * Price Increment = Cell Price

Step 4:
The final step is to draw the price values from the cardinal cross and diagonal cross into the price chart. The price values from one, or all the cardinal cross and diagonal cross angles can be used as support and resistance lines.

Step 5:
To make a forecast using these support and resistance lines, watch for a few pivots to form against the support and resistance lines. Only then can the lines be used to forecast support and resistance. The recent past will help forecast the near future. If there have been pivots on the support and resistance lines in the recent past there should be more in the near future.

CHAPTER 11: Forecasting Prices: Using a Zero Base and Overlays

This chapter shows how to forecast support and resistance prices using a Square of Nine with a zero base, an increment other than one and overlays

Example 1 - Daily Iomega, IOM

This chapter adds the use of overlays to the technique presented in Chapter 10. This method requires the selection of two numbers. The first number is an increment for advancing the Square of Nine per cell. The process to select the increment is the same as in Chapter 6. Read the section "Selecting the Increment" in Chapter 6, page 103. The second number to select is a pivot top or bottom to use in aligning the overlay's 0° angle.

Figure 119 shows a daily chart for Iomega, a company that makes computer memory devices. For this example the increment 0.25 is used and the low price of 7.48 from October 10, 2002 is used to align the overlay. The overlay's 0° angle is aligned on the low pivot price 7.48. The overlay angles of 90°, 180°, 270° and 360° are used to create support and resistance prices. As in other methods, a few pivots must form against the support and resistance lines before they can be used to forecast. On Figure 119, the pivots at A and B form on these support and resistance lines. This indicates the market favors these particular support and resistance lines and we can expect to see more pivots form against them in the future.

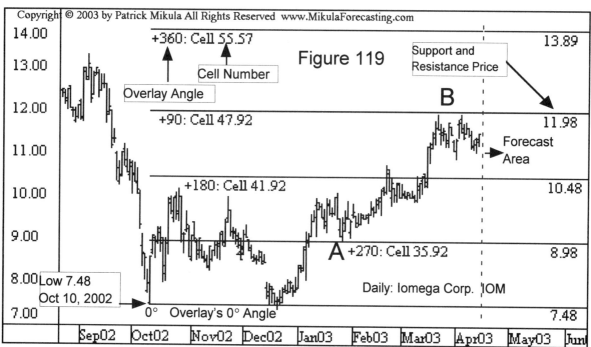

Figure 120 is the Square of Nine which corresponds with the bar chart in Figure 119. Given the price range for Iomega, an appropriate increment to use is 0.05, 0.10, 0.25 or 0.50. For the Square of Nine in Figure 120, the increment per cell is 0.25. Calculating the price values which go into each cell requires the simple formula below. For example, the price in cell 117 is calculated by, 117 *cell number* * 0.25 *increment* = 29.25 *cell price*.

Formula:
Cell Number * Price Increment = Cell Price

The overlay's 0° angle is aligned on the price 7.48 which is in cell 30. There are circles around the four support and resistance prices which are on the bar chart in Figure 119. These are the prices identified by the overlay's 90° angle, 180° angle, 270° angle and the overlay's 360° angle.

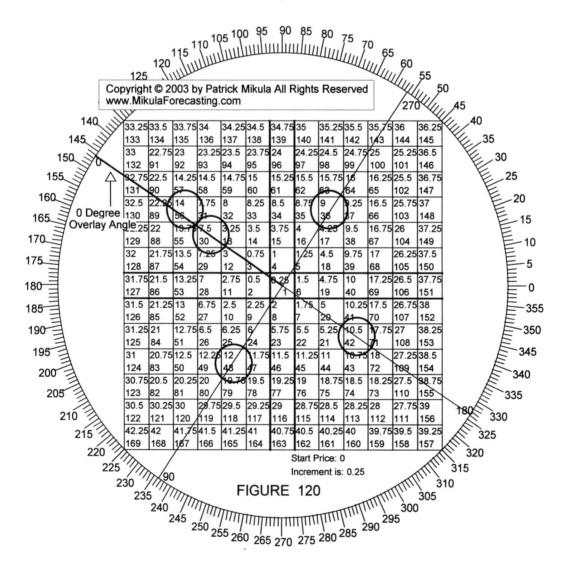

FIGURE 120

Figure 121 shows a continuation of the Iomega chart in Figure 119. After developing the pivots at A and B on these support and resistance lines, the market continues on to form a pivot bottom at point C. The pivots which formed in the recent past at A and B allow the accurate forecast of the support and resistance level at point C. Remember the recent past is the best indication of the near future.

After the top at point B, Iomega announced a $160 million drop in revenue from the previous year. This caused the stock price to fall down to the support line and make the bottom at point C.

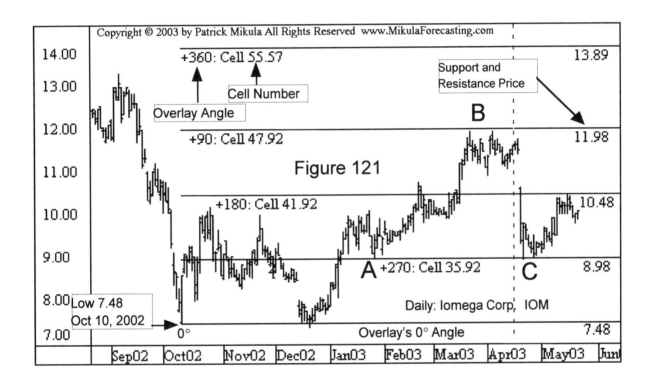

Example 2 of Forecasting Support and Resistance Levels Using a Zero Base and an Overlay: Daily Wellpoint Health Network, WLP

Figure 122 shows a daily bar chart for Wellpoint Health Network, symbol WLP. To apply this technique to a chart, two numbers must be selected. The first number is the increment per cell used to advance the prices of the Square of Nine. Based on the WLP price range, 0.5 is used as the increment. The second number to select is the price of a high or low pivot. In this example the top pivot of 89.20 from October 17, 2002 is used.

After calculating all the prices for the Square of Nine, the overlay's 0° angle is aligned on the pivot price 89.20. This is on Figure 122. The overlay angles 90°, 180°, 270° and 360° are used to generate support and resistance price levels. On the left end of each support and resistance line is the overlay angle and the cell number where the price is located. On the right end of each line is the price at which the line is drawn.

On Figure 122, the price falls from the overlay's starting price of 89.20. It stops at the support line labeled, -360: Cell 129. The label, -360: Cell 129, indicates the support line is the overlay's 0°/360° angle and the line price can be found in cell 129. The actual line price is listed as 64.53. The price of Wellpoint makes two bottom pivots on this line at A and B.

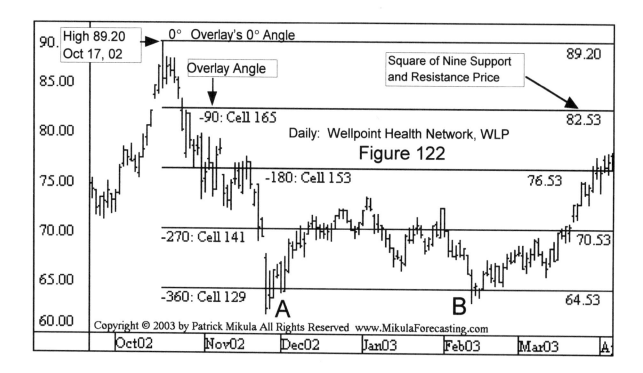

Figure 123 is the Square of Nine which corresponds with the chart in Figure 122. For the Square of Nine in Figure 123, the increment per cell is 0.50. Calculating the price values which go into each cell requires the formula below. For example, the price in cell 197 is calculated by, 197 *cell number* * 0.50 *increment* = 98.50 *cell price*.

> **Formula:**
> Cell Number * Price Increment = Cell Price

The overlay's 0° angle is aligned on the price 89.20 which is in cell 178. There are circles around the support and resistance prices which are on the chart in Figure 122. These are the prices identified by the overlay's 90° angle, 180° angle, 270° angle and the overlay's 360° angle.

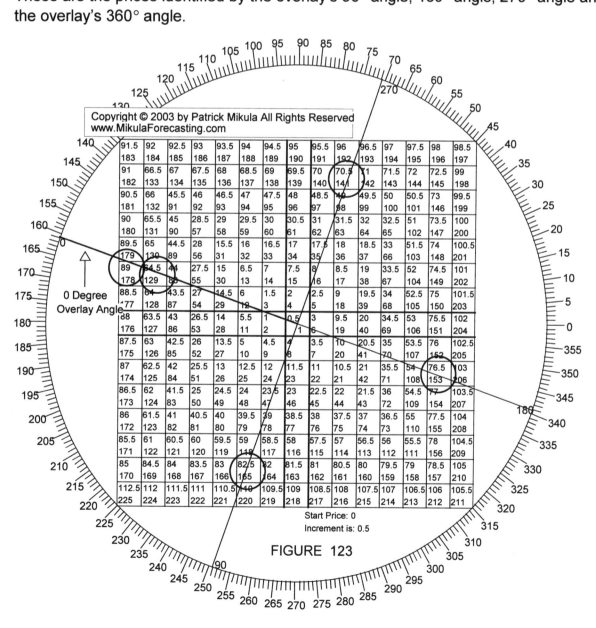

FIGURE 123

Chapter 11 Review

Objective:
Forecast support and resistance levels.

Step 1:
Set the Square of Nine starting price to zero.

Step 2:
Select a price increment which is not equal to one. Chapter 6 and this chapter use the same process to select a price increment. Read the section "Selecting the Increment" in Chapter 6, page 103. The price increment is used to advance the Square of Nine starting price one increment per cell.

Step 3:
Select a pivot top or bottom price which will be used to align the overlay's 0° angle.

Step 4:
Calculate the price which goes into each Square of Nine cell by multiplying the cell number by the increment. Use the formula below.

```
Formula:
Cell Number * Price Increment = Cell Price
```

Step 5:
Draw the price values from the overlay angles on to the price chart. The price values from one, or all the overlay angles, can be used as support and resistance lines.

Step 6:
To make a forecast using these support and resistance lines, watch for a few pivots to form against the support and resistance lines. Only then can the lines be used to forecast support and resistance. The recent past will help forecast the near future. If there have been pivots on the support and resistance lines in the recent past there most likely will be more in the near future.

CHAPTER 12: Forecasting Dates: Using Shape Overlays

This chapter shows how to forecast pivot dates using a Square of Nine and shape overlays

Example 1 - Daily Wheat

One of the oldest forecasting techniques W.D.Gann used is based on divisions of the year. W.D.Gann aligned one of the shape overlays to a date found on the outer ring of the Square of Nine. The corners of the shape overlay are then aligned on the dates which divide the year. The starting dates W.D.Gann used were the dates of high and low pivots. Figure 124 shows a daily chart for Wheat futures. This example uses the octagon shape overlay which divides the year into eight sections of 45°. The overlay has been aligned on the low pivot date 12/30/2002. The dates identified by the first four corners of the octagon overlay are shown.

Before a forecast can be made with this method, one or two of the dates identifies by the shape overlay must correlate with a pivot point. If the dates identified by the shape overlay do not correlate with historical pivots then no forecast is possible.

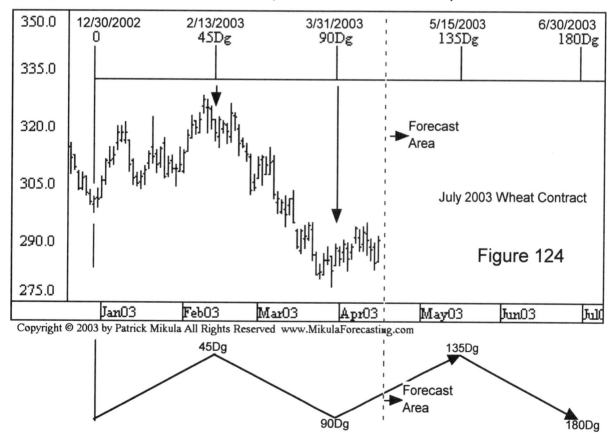
Figure 124

Figure 124 shows that the date 2/13/2003 identified by the 45° corner of the octagon shape overlay correlates with a pivot top. The 90° corner of the octagon shape overlay identified the date 3/31/2003 which is near a pivot bottom. Because the first two octagon corners correlate with pivots, a forecast can be made that the future dates identified by the octagon corners will also correlate with market pivots.

Figure 125 shows the Square of Nine with the dates around the outside. The dates are listed every 15°. The 0° start corner is aligned on the starting date 12/30/2002. The 45° corner identifies 2/13/2003, the 90° corner identifies 3/31/2003, the 135° corner identifies 5/15/2003 and the 180° corner identifies 6/30/2003.

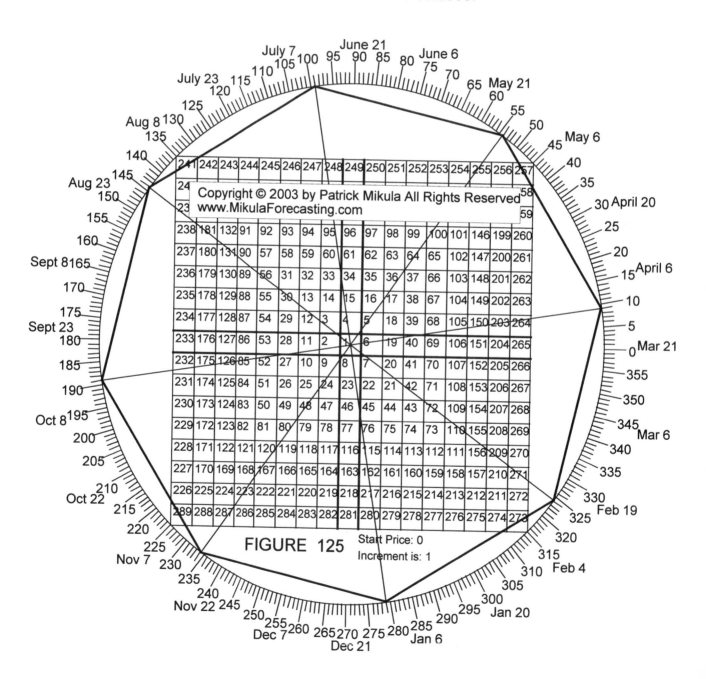

FIGURE 125

Figure 126 shows the Wheat market which was shown previously in Figure 124. Notice at point A on Figure 126, the market moves up to the 135° date 5/15/2003 and makes a top.

Notice the line diagram below the price chart on Figure 126. This diagram shows the top bottom sequence of the pivots identified by the octagon shape overlay. If these dates stay in sequence, then the next pivot date can be forecast as a top or bottom. For example on Figure 124, the starting date was a bottom, the 45Dg date was a top and then the 90Dg date was a bottom. This shows a bottom, top, bottom sequence. Then the 135Dg date could be forecast as a top and the 180Dg date could be forecast as a bottom. If there is no top bottom sequence, the 135Dg date could still be forecast as a pivot date but it would not be forecast as a top.

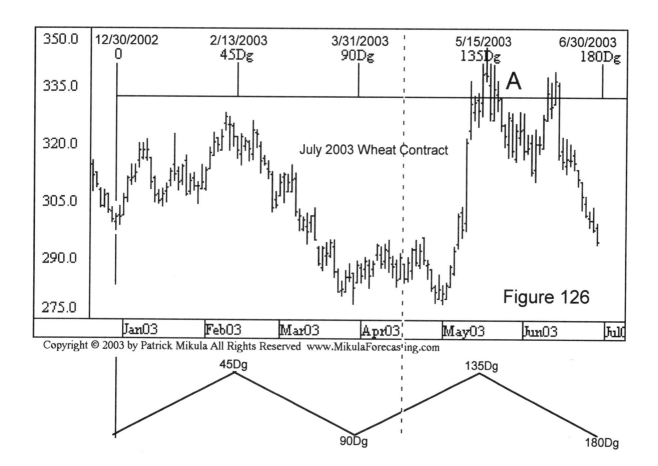

Example 2 of Forecasting Pivot Dates Using Shape Overlays: 5 Minute Minnesota Mining & Manufacturing Co., MMM

Here is an intraday example of forecasting pivots using a shape overlay. Figure 127 shows a 5 minute bar chart for Minnesota Mining & Manufacturing, symbol MMM. When W.D.Gann placed time on the outer ring of the Square of Nine he used the 24 hours of one day. This is not the time period we will use on the outer ring for this method. When using the full 24 hours, most of the forecast times occur when the market is not open. This example will use 9:30 am to 4:00 pm when the market is open as the time around the outer ring of the Square of Nine.

Figure 127 shows the times identified by aligning the square shape overlay on the pivot high time 12:15 pm, June 9. Before a forecast can be made, some of the historical pivot times identified by the square overlay have to correlate with pivots. On Figure 127, the 90Dg time is near a pivot top and the 180Dg time is near a pivot bottom. Based on this, the forecast can be made that the next times identified by the square shape overlay will also correlate with a pivot.

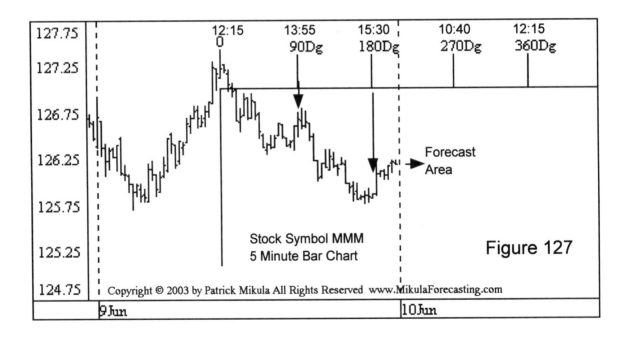

Figure 128 shows a Square of Nine with the trading hours for the New Your Stock Exchange around the outside. The 0° corner of the square overlay is aligned on 12:15. The 90° corner of the square, lines up with 13:55, the 180° corner lines up with 15:30 and the 270° corner lines us with 10:40.

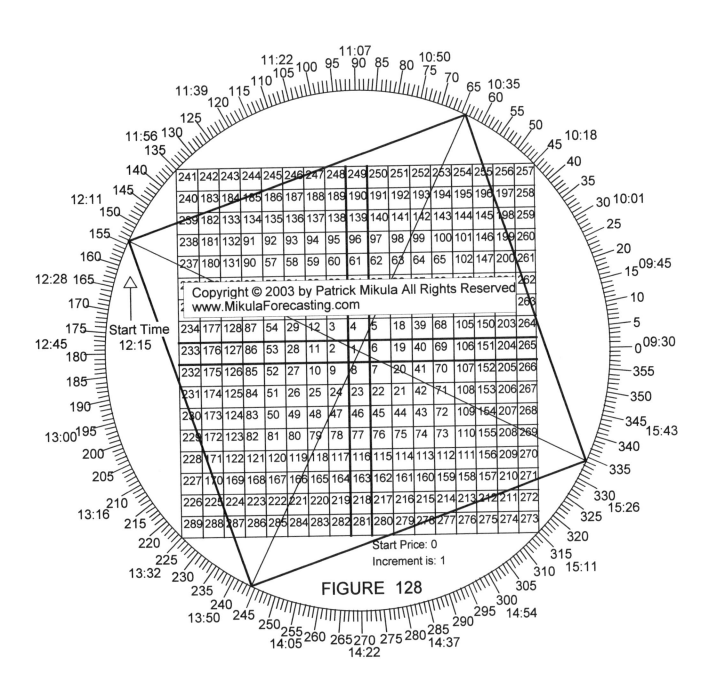

FIGURE 128

Figure 129 shows the 5 minute chart for MMM. The forecast time of 10:40 is near a pivot bottom at A. The forecast time 12:15 is near a pivot top at B.

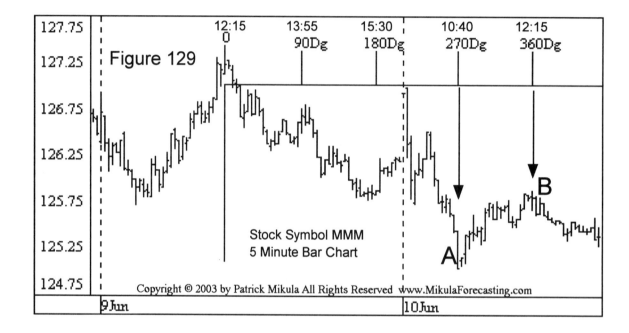

Example 3 of Forecasting Pivot Dates Using Shape Overlays:
5 Minute Disney, DIS

This example will use a 5 minute bar chart for Disney, symbol DIS. The hours of trading for the New York Stock Exchange. 9:30 am to 4:00 pm are again placed around the outside of the Square of Nine. Figure 130 shows the times identified by the triangle overlay when it is aligned to the time 11:15. Before a forecast can be made, at least one of the historical times must correlate with a pivot. On Figure 130, the 240Dg time of 15:35 is near a pivot top. After this occurs, a forecast is made for the next time identified by the triangle overlay. This is the 360Dg time or 11:15 am.

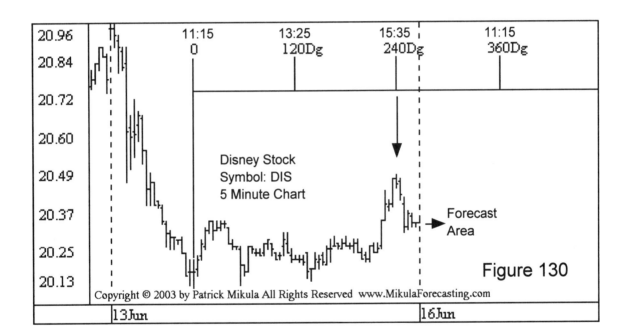

Figure 130

Figure 131 shows the 0° point of the triangle overlay aligned on 11:15 am. The 120° point of the triangle overlay identifies 13:25. The 240° point of the triangle overlay lines up with 15:35.

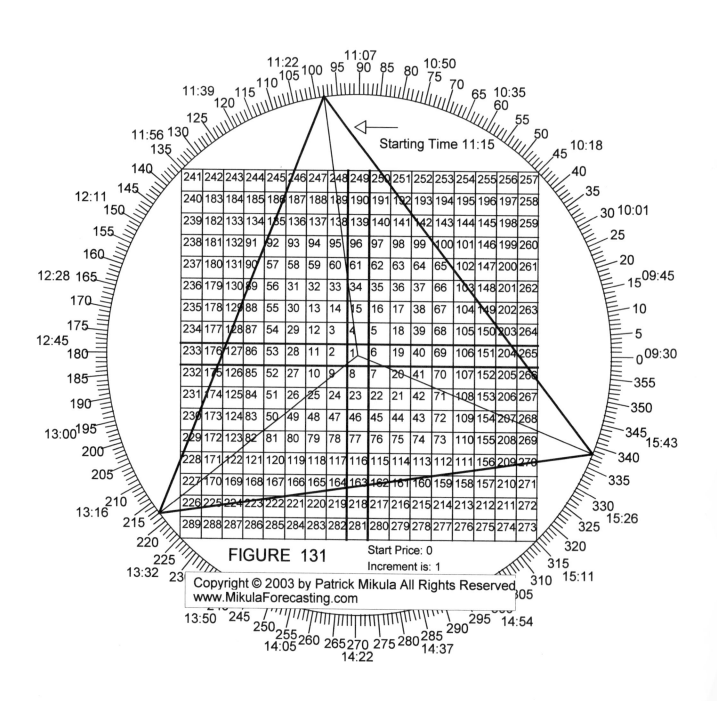

FIGURE 131

The chart in Figure 132, shows a continuation of the 5 minute bar chart for Disney. The price moves up and makes a top at the forecast time 11:15 at point A.

In this example and the previous intraday example, the market makes a top at a forecast time which is 360° from the starting time. This means a pivot formed at the same time the next day. When using this method with an intraday chart, always watch the 360° point for pivots because it has a greater tendency to form a pivot than any other time.

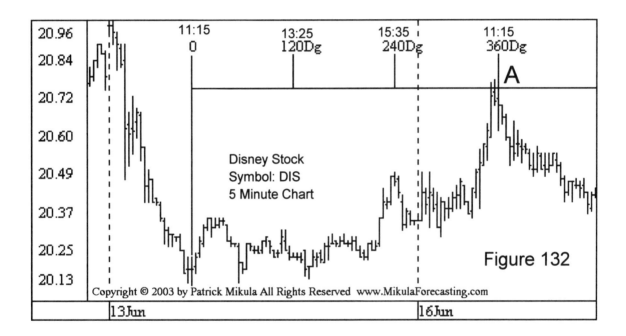

Figure 132

Chapter 12 Review

Objective:
Forecast the date or time of pivots.

Step 1:
Align one of the shape overlays to a pivot date on the Square of Nine.

Step 2:
Identify the dates which line up with the corners of the shape overlay. Look for some of the historical dates to correlate with pivots. If some of the historical dates do line up with pivots, then the next dates in the sequence can be used to forecast pivots.

Step 3:
If the historical pivots which correlate with the overlay dates have maintained the top, bottom, top, bottom sequence, then the next pivot should continue the sequence. The next pivot is then forecast as either a top or bottom. If there is no top bottom sequence, the overlay dates can still be used to forecast a pivot but not a specific top or bottom.

Step 4:
When using this forecasting method on an intraday chart, pay special attention to the 360° forecast time.

CHAPTER 13: Price and Time Forecasting Grid #1

*This chapter shows how to create and use
Price and Time Forecasting Grid #1*

How to Create and Use, Price and Time Forecasting Grid #1

In this book, Chapters 2 through 12 describe eleven methods for forecasting prices or pivot dates. By using a price forecasting method and a time forecasting method on the same chart, a Price and Time Forecasting Grid is created. The price forecasting method creates a set of horizontal lines and the time forecasting method creates a set of vertical lines. These horizontal and vertical lines create the Price and Time Forecasting Grid. The Price and Time Forecasting Grid #1 is created by using the price forecasting method in Chapter 3 and a fixed time cycle forecasting method.

The chart in Figure 133 is a daily chart for the Commodity Research Bureau index which is also know as the CRB commodity index. The price forecasting method described in Chapter 3 has been applied to this chart. The starting price for the Square of Nine overlay is the February 24, 2003 high price of 251.59. Price lines representing each 45° of movement on the Square of Nine are added to this chart. These price lines are the first step to create the Price and Time Forecasting Grid #1.

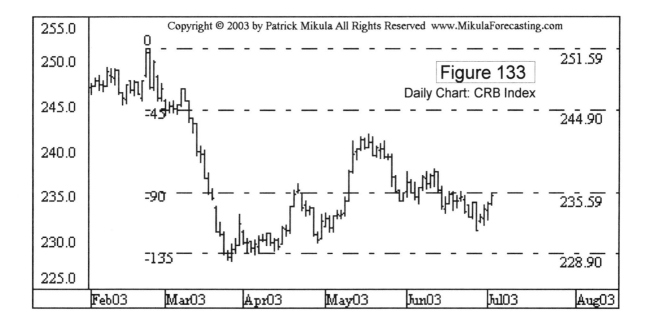

Step 2 for creating the Price and Time Forecasting Grid #1, is to add the vertical time lines. On Figure 134, the price of the CRB commodity index falls from the top starting point and makes a bottom on the price line which is -135° around the Square of Nine. This bottom is identified by the letter A. This bottom, at point A, is 21 bars from the starting bar. In this example, the time of 21 bars is used as the fixed time cycle size. The vertical lines are 21 bars apart. This creates increments of 21, 42, 63, 84 and so on. Any size can be used for the fixed cycle time lines. When selecting the cycle size the time from the starting point to the first significant pivot should always be considered as a possible candidate for the cycle size.

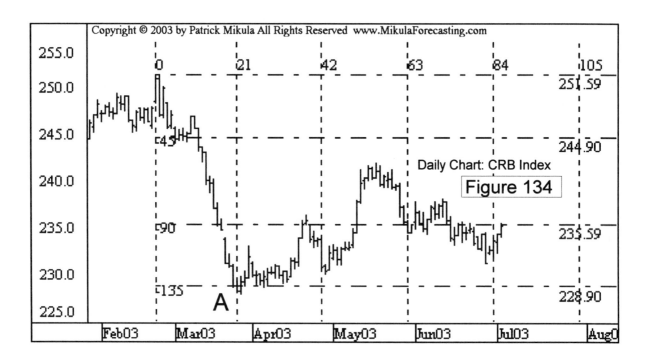

The third step to create the Price and Time Forecasting Grid #1 is to connect the intersections of the horizontal price line and the vertical time lines with upward sloping lines. On Figure 135, upward sloping lines are drawn connecting the intersections of the price and time lines.

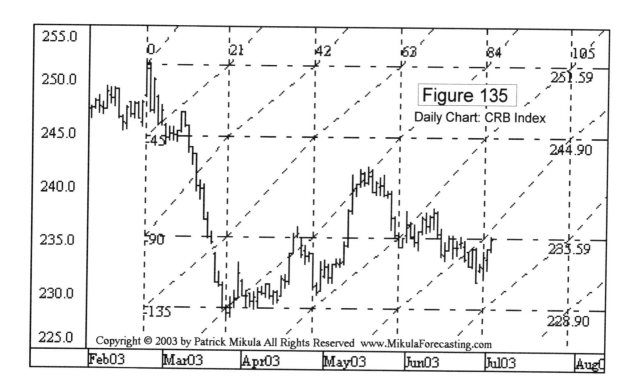
Figure 135
Daily Chart: CRB Index

The fourth and final step to create the Price and Time Forecasting Grid #1, is to connect the intersections of the horizontal price line and the vertical time lines with downward sloping lines. On Figure 136, downward sloping lines are drawn connecting the intersections of the price and time lines. Figure 136 shows the complete Price and Time Forecasting Grid #1.

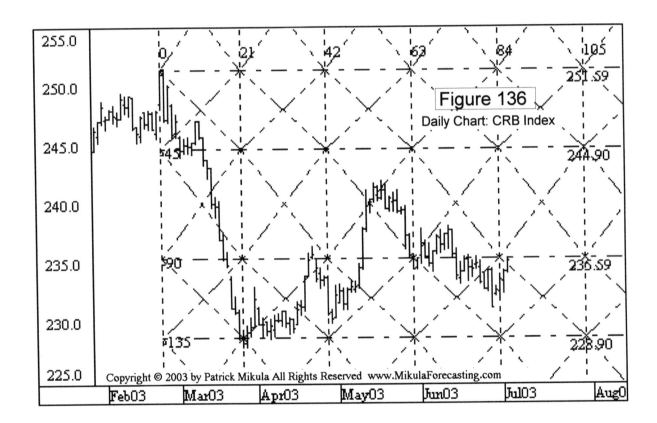

Figure 136
Daily Chart: CRB Index

Example 1 of the Price and Time Forecasting Grid #1: Daily CRB Commodity Index

Figure 137 shows the daily CRB commodity index with the Price and Time Forecasting Grid #1 applied to the chart. Point A on Figure 137, is the measuring point for the time cycles. Point A is 21 bars past the starting point so all the vertical time lines are 21 bars apart. The horizontal price lines are forecast by the method in Chapter 3.

After point A, the price moves up to point B where a top forms on the -90° price line. The price then falls until it reaches the second vertical time line at point C. When the price reaches the time line at C, there is a fast move up to point D. Point D is right above the intersection of two diagonal lines. The intersection of two lines is always an important location to watch for a pivot to form. At point D, the price reaches the intersection of two diagonal lines and forms a top pivot. The price then falls to point E and makes a small bottom pivot at the intersection of a horizontal price line and a vertical time line. Finally the price falls to point F and makes a bottom just before a vertical time line. The Price and Time Forecasting Grid works as a road map for the pivots as they unfold. The review at the end of this chapter includes a list of items to watch for when using the Price and Time Forecasting Grid.

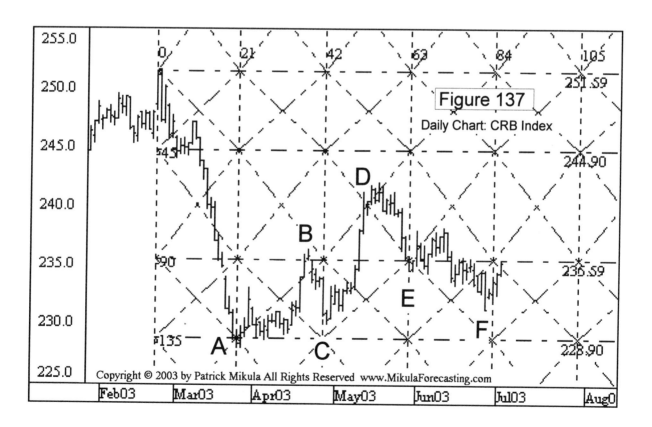

Figure 138 shows the same CRB index chart in Figure 137. The diagonal lines in the Price and Time Forecasting Grid commonly work as a price channel. Watch for this to happen. On Figure 138, there are four arrows, two point up and two point down. The two upward arrows mark the boundaries of an upward price channel created by the Price and Time Forecasting Grid. Notice that the price stays between the top and bottom boundary of this channel as it moves up from point A to point B.

The two downward sloping arrows identify the boundaries of a downward price channel created by the Price and Time Forecasting Grid. After the top at point B, the price falls and stays inside the boundaries of this price channel.

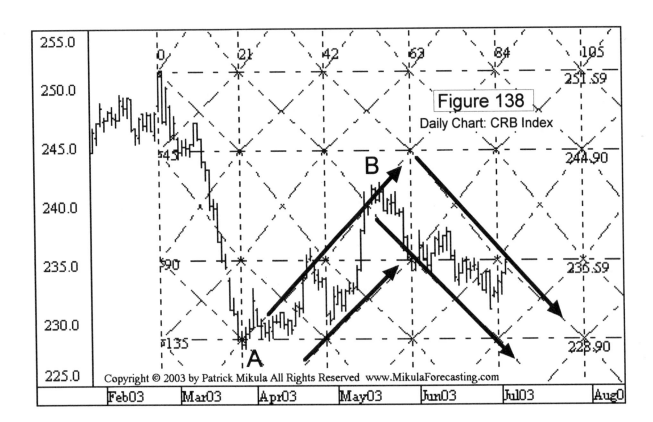

Example 2 for the Price and Time Forecasting Grid #1:
15 Minute Amazon.com AMZN

Figure 139 shows a 15 minute bar chart for Amazon.com stock. The lines are drawn for the Price and Time Forecasting Grid #1. The horizontal price lines are created by using the method in Chapter 3. The starting point for the grid is the low price of 34.54 on June 24, 2003, 10:15 am. This is an intraday chart with a low price scale. The starting price is multiplied by 100 so it can be used on the Square of Nine to create the price lines.

The top at point A, is the time cycle measuring point. From the starting bar to point A, there are 28 bars. Each time cycle line is 28 bars apart.

After point A, the price falls to point B and makes a bottom on the +90° price line. Then the price moves sideways until it reaches point C at the second vertical time line. At point C, the price starts a fast break upward. The price moves up until at point D it makes a top at the intersection of the +360° price line and the third time line.

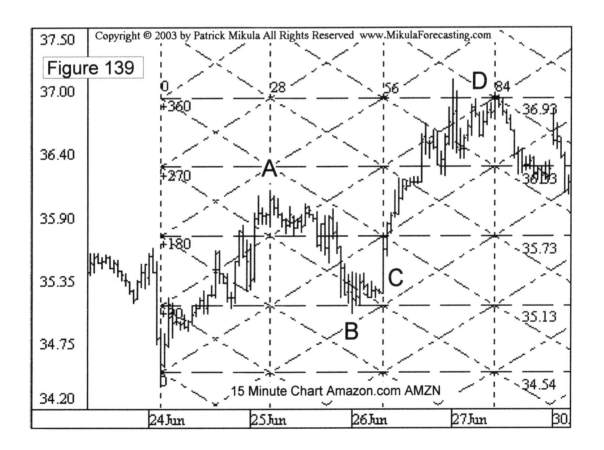

Figure 140 is a continuation of the 15 minute Amazon.com chart in Figure 139. After the top at point D, the price falls to point E and forms a bottom on the +180° price line. The price then moves sideways. When it reaches the fifth time line, it starts a fast move up at point F. Finally the price moves up and makes a top at point G against the next higher +180° price line. The Price and Time Forecasting Grid lays a mapping grid onto the price chart. In a great many cases, it helps a trader or forecaster identify pivots as they occur.

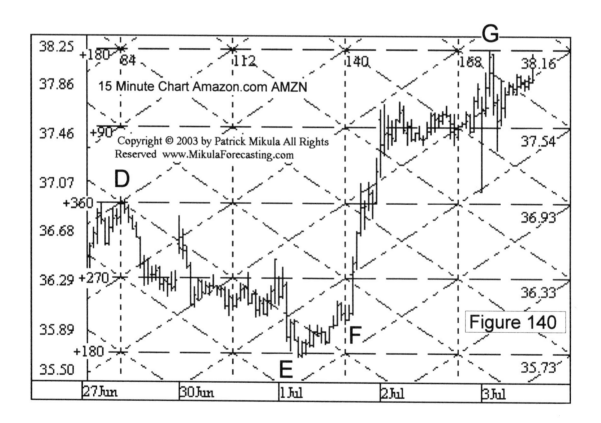

Figure 140

Chapter 13 Review

Objective:
Use the Price and Time Forecasting Grid #1 to identify pivots as they occur.

Step 1:
Use the method in Chapter 3 to draw the horizontal price lines.

Step 2:
Draw the vertical time lines on the chart. The time line spacing is a fixed cycle size. A common cycle size to use for the time cycle is the time between the starting point used in step 1 and the first significant pivot. This is the method used to determine the cycle size in the two examples in this chapter.

Step 3:
Complete the Price and Time Forecasting Grid #1 by drawing the upward and downward sloping lines. These lines connect the vertical and horizontal line intersections.

Step 4:
As the price unfolds through Price and Time Forecasting Grid #1, watch for the following items.

1.) Watch for pivots to form against price lines.

2.) Watch for pivots to form when the price reaches a time line.

3.) Watch for a fast break to start from a time line.

4.) Watch for pivots to form when the price reaches an intersection between a horizontal price line and a vertical time line.

5.) Watch for pivots to form when the price reaches an intersection between two diagonal lines.

6.) Watch for the upward diagonal lines to form an upward price channel.

7.) Watch for the downward diagonal lines to form a downward price channel.

CHAPTER 14: Price and Time Forecasting Grid #2

*This chapter shows how to create and use
Price and Time Forecasting Grid #2*

How to Create and Use, Price and Time Forecasting Grid #2

Price and Time Forecasting Grid #2 is created by using a price forecasting method and a time forecasting method on a chart simultaneously. The method in Chapter 3 is used to create the horizontal price lines. The method in Chapter 4 is used to create the vertical time lines.

Step 1 to create Price and Time Forecasting Grid #2 is to draw the price lines on a chart using the method in Chapter 3. Figure 141 shows a weekly chart for the S&P500. The price forecasting method in Chapter 3 is applied with the starting date of March 24, 2000 at the top price 1552.87. This is the all time high for the S&P500. The horizontal price lines are drawn every 360° moved around the Square of Nine.

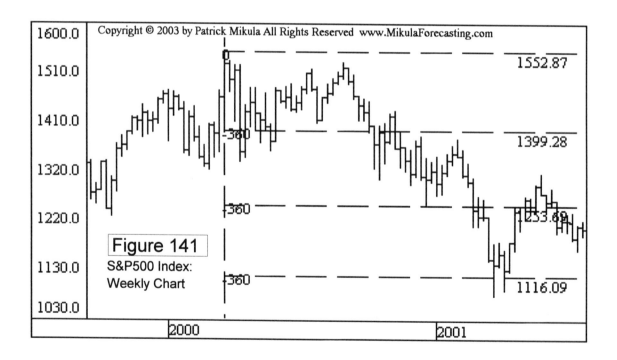

Step 2 is to draw the time lines on the price chart using the method in Chapter 4. This method draws time lines based on the Square of Nine cell numbers found on the diagonal cross and cardinal cross. On Figure 142, the first vertical time line is labeled 23, and marks the exact bar of the first top pivot after the starting bar. On the Square of Nine, the number 23 is on the 270° angle which is the downward vertical angle in the cardinal cross. Because the 270° angle in the cardinal cross identifies the first pivot, this angle is used to create all the vertical time lines.

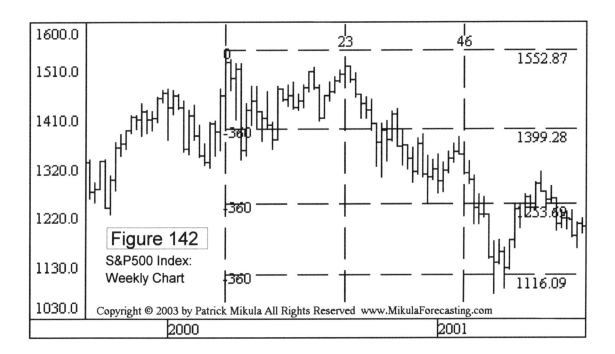

The third step to create the Price and Time Forecasting Grid #2 is to draw the upward angles. These angles connect the intersections of the horizontal price lines and the vertical time lines. See Figure 143.

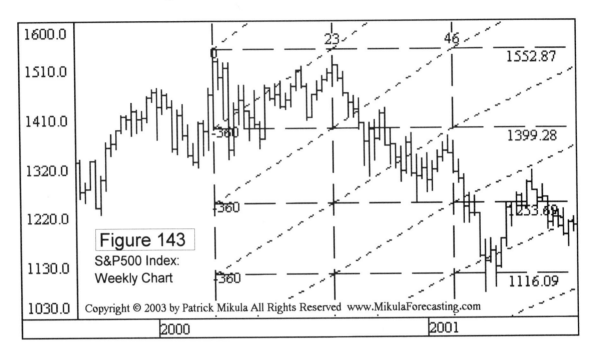

The 4th and final step to create the Price and Time Forecasting Grid #2 is to draw the downward angles. These angles also connect the intersections of the horizontal price lines and the vertical time lines. See Figure 144.

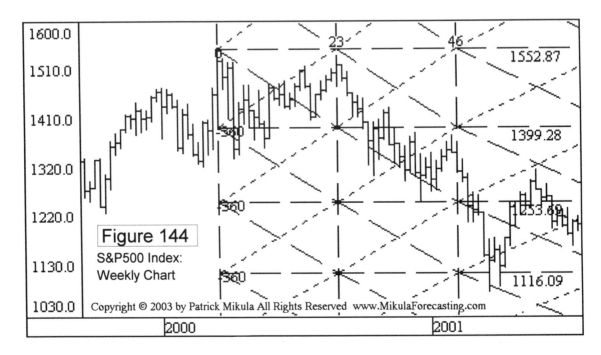

Example 1 of the Price and Time Forecasting Grid #2: Weekly S&P500 Index

This first example of Price and Time Grid #2 uses the Weekly chart for the S&P500. This is the same chart that is on the previous three pages. The starting bar for creating the grid is the all time high for the S&P500, March 24, 2000 at the price of 1552.87. The method in Chapter 3 is applied to create the price lines and the method in Chapter 4 is applied to create the time lines. The vertical time lines are drawn based on the cell numbers on the 270° angle on the Square of Nine. This is the lower vertical angle on the cardinal cross. The diagonal lines have the appearance of being slightly curved because the time lines progressively farther apart.

When selecting the Square of Nine angle to use to create the time line, you should look for the closest match to the first pivot after the starting bar. On Figure 145 the first time line labeled A, also labeled 23, exactly marks the first swing top bar after the starting bar. The label 23 is the cell number from the Square of Nine. Cell 23 is on the 270° angle on the cardinal cross. This is why this cardinal cross angle is selected for constructing the time lines.

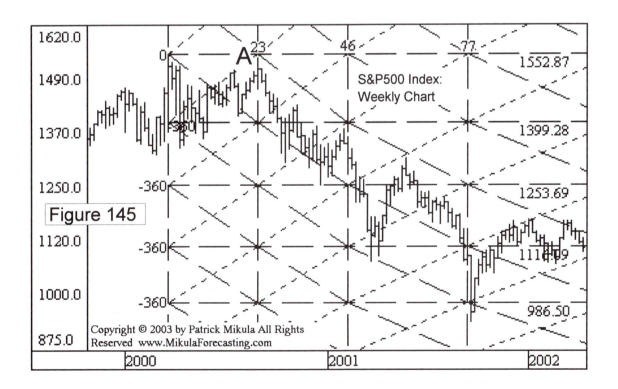

Figure 146 shows the same S&P500 chart in Figure 145. On Figure 146, two of the downward sloping lines are highlighted. These two angles create a downward price channel. As the S&P500 moves down through 2000, 2001 and 2002, it makes tops and bottoms against this price channel. The tops at point B, D, F and G all form on the top channel line. The two bottoms at C and E form on the bottom channel line.

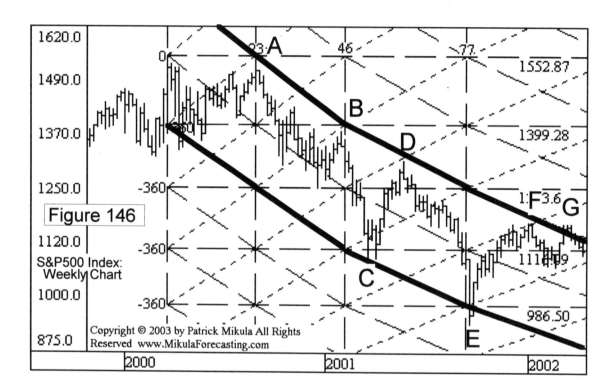

Figure 147 is a continuation of the chart on Figure 146. After the top at point G, the price falls and makes a double bottom on the lower channel line at points H and I. The market is currently up to point J and is again on the upper channel line. If this bear market in the S&P500 is going to continue, it must make a break downward. If the S&P500 moves above the upper channel then the bear market which started in 2000 will be over.

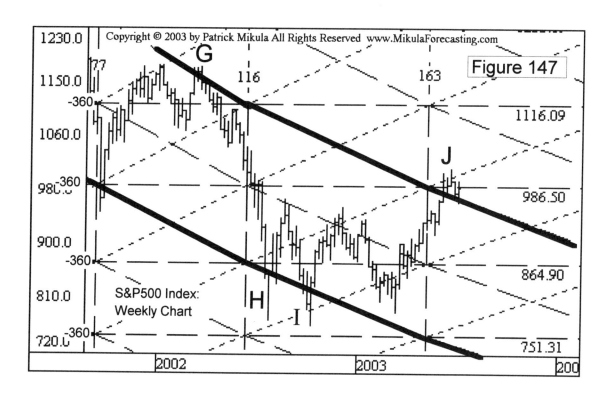

Example 2 of the Price and Time Forecasting Grid #2:
15 Minute Symantec Corp., SYMC

Figure 148 shows a 15 minute chart for the software company, Symantec, SYMC. On this chart, the horizontal price lines are created using the method in Chapter 3. The starting point is the high price of 46.50 on June 25, 2003 at 14:00. Using the method in Chapter 3, the price lines are drawn every 90° away from the starting price. This is an intraday chart with a small price range and low prices therefore the starting price is multiplied by 100 so it can be used on the Square of Nine.

The vertical time lines are created using the method in Chapter 4. The first bottom pivot after the starting bar is identified by point A. This pivot bar is 19 bars away from the starting bar. The Square of Nine cell 19 is on the 0° angle of the cardinal cross. This is the right side horizontal angle of the cardinal cross. Because this angle identifies the first pivot after the starting bar, it is used to calculate all the time lines.

After point A, the price falls to the bottom at point B and makes a bottom on the -360° price line. Next the price moves up to point C and makes a top at the intersection of the second time line and the -180° price line. After point C, the price falls and makes a bottom at point D on the second -90° price line.

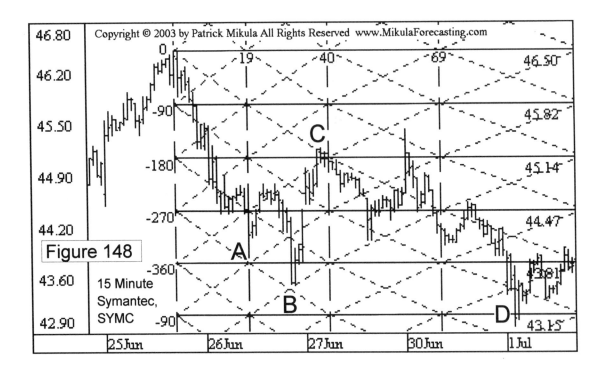

Figure 149 is a continuation of Figure 148. After the bottom at point D, the price rallies and makes a top at the intersection of the 106 time line and the -270° price line, at point E. Next the price falls and makes another bottom on the -90° price line at point F. Finally the price again moves up and makes a double top on the -270° price line at points G and H. It is very common to see the price move between the price lines forming several pivots in a row on different price lines and at the intersections of price and time lines.

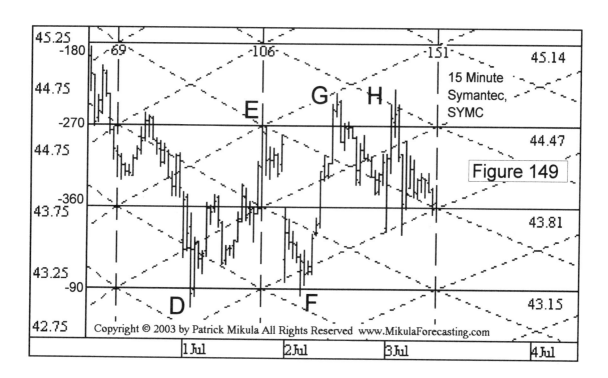

Chapter 14 Review

Objective:
Use the Price and Time Forecasting Grid #2 to identify pivots as they occur.

Step 1:
Use the method in Chapter 3 to draw the horizontal price lines.

Step 2:
Use the method in Chapter 4 to draw the vertical time lines on the chart. A common way to select the Square of Nine angle used in creating the time lines, is to find the angle on the Square of Nine diagonal cross or cardinal cross which produces the closest match to the first pivot after the starting bar. This is the method used in the two examples in this chapter.

Step 3:
Complete the Price and Time Forecasting Grid #2 by drawing the upward and downward sloping lines. These lines connect the vertical and horizontal line intersections.

Step 4:
As the price unfolds through Price and Time Forecasting Grid #2, watch for the following items.

1.) Watch for pivots to form against price lines.

2.) Watch for pivots to form when the price reaches a time line.

3.) Watch for a fast break to start from the time line.

4.) Watch for pivots to form when the price reaches an intersection between a horizontal price line and a vertical time line.

5.) Watch for pivots to form when the price reaches an intersection between two diagonal lines.

6.) Watch for the upward diagonal lines to form an upward price channel.

7.) Watch for the downward diagonal lines to form a downward price channel.

CHAPTER 15: Mikula's Square of Nine Planetary Angles

This chapter shows how to draw planetary angles based on the Square of Nine.

How to Draw Mikula's Square of Nine Planetary Angles

This chapter shows a method which I developed almost 10 years ago in 1994. Since that time this method has proved to be just about the best way to use planetary data for trading. These planetary angles have shown themselves to be accurate in locating pivot price levels as well as being easy to understand.

To convert a planetary longitude to a price which can be drawn on a chart, start by looking up the longitude for the planet on a specific day. On March 27, 2003 the geocentric longitude for Mars was 284.0°. The second step is to locate this degree on the outer ring around the Square of Nine. This can been seen in Figure 151. The symbol for Mars ♂ is located at 284° and is circled. To locate the prices which are affiliated with this longitude, place the overlay's 0° angle on this degree. In Figure 151 the overlay has been aligned to the degree 284° on the outer ring around the Square of Nine. The prices you will place on the price chart for this date March 27, 2003 are the prices which are on the overlay's 0° angle.

Figure 150 is a chart for the S&P500. There are two prices on the overlay's 0° angle which fall in the price range of the S&P500 chart. These are 942 and 823. Figure 150 shows these prices drawn on the S&P500 chart for March 27, 2003.

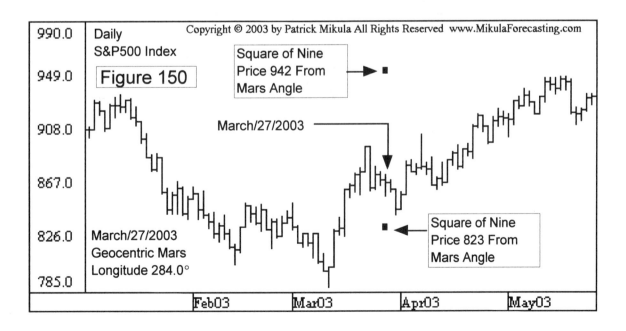

Figure 151 shows the overlay's 0° angle aligned on the longitude of Mars ♂ 284° form March 27, 2003. The circled prices on the Square of Nine, 942 and 823 are the two prices which fall in the price range of the S&P500. This process is repeated for each bar on the chart to calculate a price for each bar. When all the prices are drawn on the chart, it creates a set of angles which represent the Square of Nine values for the planet Mars.

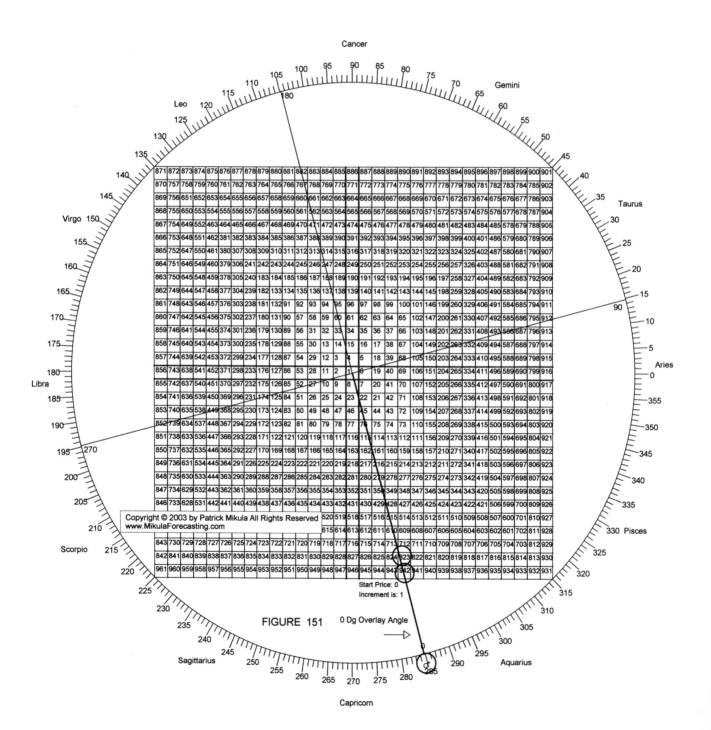

FIGURE 151

Figure 152 shows the S&P500 chart after this process is repeated for every bar on the chart. The two angles on the S&P500 chart represent the planetary angles for geocentric Mars from the overlay's 0° angle.

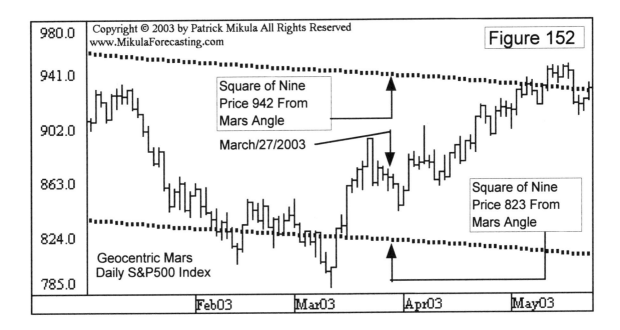

This process can be repeated for the other angles on the overlay. Figure 153 shows two additional angles which are calculated using the overlay's 180° angle.

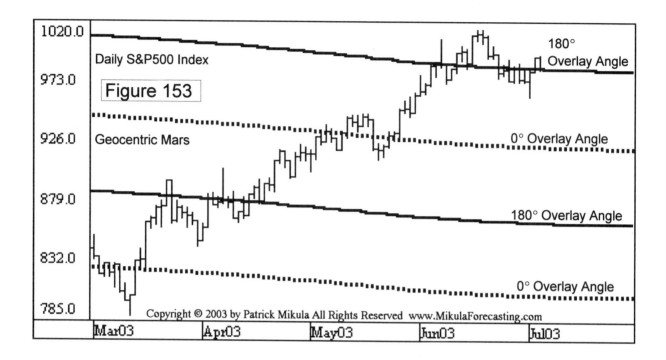

Figure 154 shows the angles for geocentric Mars which are calculated using the overlay's +90° angle and -90° angle.

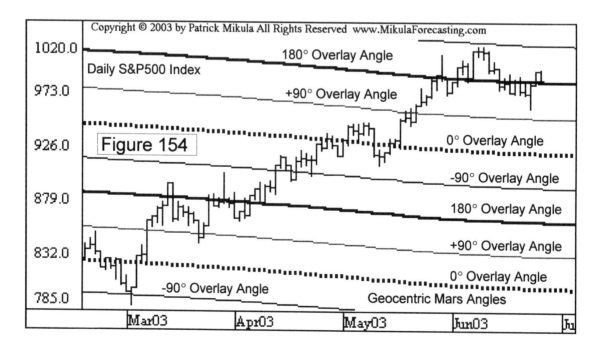

On Figures 152, 153 and 154, the planetary angles are sloping downward. This is because the numbers on the Square of Nine move clock wise while the degrees on the outer ring around the square move counter-clock wise. It is possible to invert the angles so they move upward. Figure 155 shows an S&P500 chart with the geocentric Mars angles now drawn inverted so they slope upward.

This introduction has used geocentric Mars but it is, of course, possible to use any of the planets with this method.

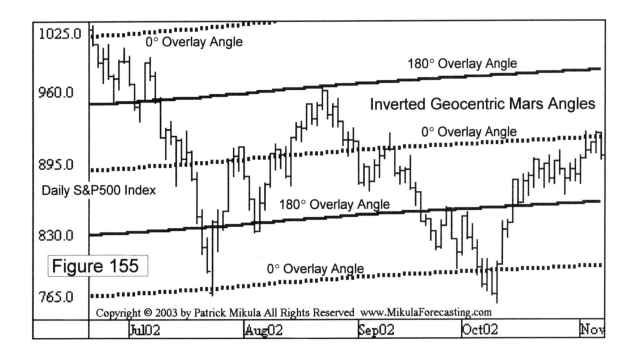

Example 1 of Mikula's Square of Nine Planetary Angles: Daily NASDAQ Index

Figure 156 shows the daily NASDAQ index. The planetary angles drawn on this chart are the inverted geocentric Mars angles from the overlay's 0° angle and 180° angle. The prices based on the overlay's 0° angle are drawn as heavy lines. The prices based on the overlay's 180° angle are drawn as thin lines.

Figure 156 shows that a lot of market pivots have formed on these planetary angles. There are pivot bottoms on these planetary angles at points A, B, C, E, G and I. There are pivot tops on these planetary angles at points D, F, H, J and K.

It is common for a market to start a swing on one planetary angle and end the swing on the next higher planetary angle which is calculated with the same overlay angle. For example, notice that a swing starts at the bottom point E, on a planetary angle calculated with the 0° overlay angle. The market then moves up to the next higher planetary angle at point F, which is also calculated with the 0° angle. This occurs again between two angles calculated with the 180° overlay angle as the price moves from point I to J.

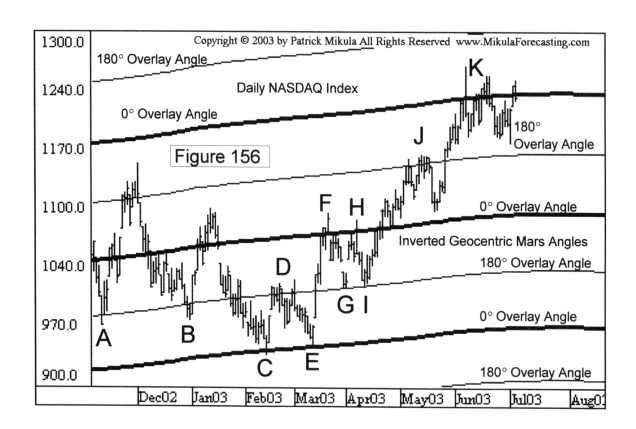

Example 2 of Mikula's Square of Nine Planetary Angles:
Daily Euro-Currency

This example uses a futures contract for the Euro-Currency Unit which has a very low price scale. This chart price scale can be seen in Figure 157.

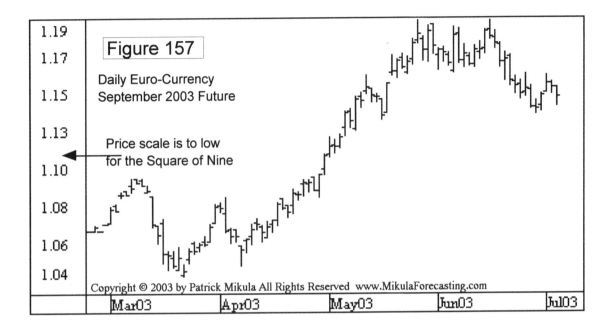

To use a financial instrument with a low price scale, the price scale can be multiplied by 100. Figure 158 shows the same Euro-Currency chart in Figure 157 except the price scale has been multiplied by 100 to create higher price values.

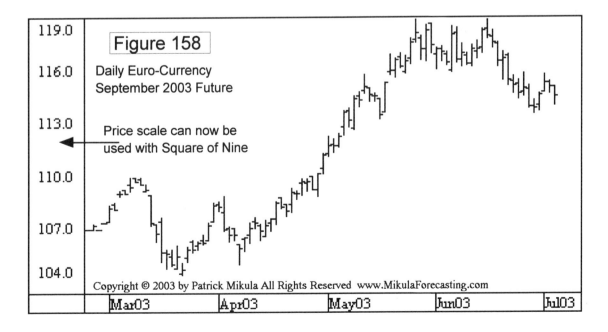

Figure 159 shows the Euro-Currency chart with the higher price scale. The inverted planetary angles for geocentric Mars are added to this chart. The angles on this chart are calculated using the overlay's 0° angle, +90° angle, 180° angle and -90° angle.

Figure 159 shows this market makes a bottom on the -90° planetary angle at point A. Then the market moves up and makes a top slightly below the next higher -90° planetary angle at point B. It is a common occurrence for a market to move between two planetary angles calculated with the same overlay angle.

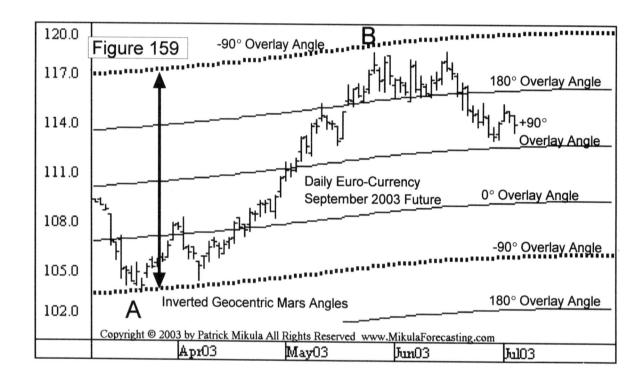

Example 3 of Mikula's Square of Nine Planetary Angles:
Daily Soybean Futures

Figure 160 shows a chart for November 2003 Soybeans. The inverted planetary angles for Heliocentric Jupiter are added to the chart. The planetary angles are calculated with the overlay's 0° angle and the overlay's 180° angle. Tops form on these angles at points A, B, D and E. A bottom forms on the 180° angle at point C. These angles are very easy to use and have stood the test of time. They can consistently locate prices where pivots form if they are drawn on a chart.

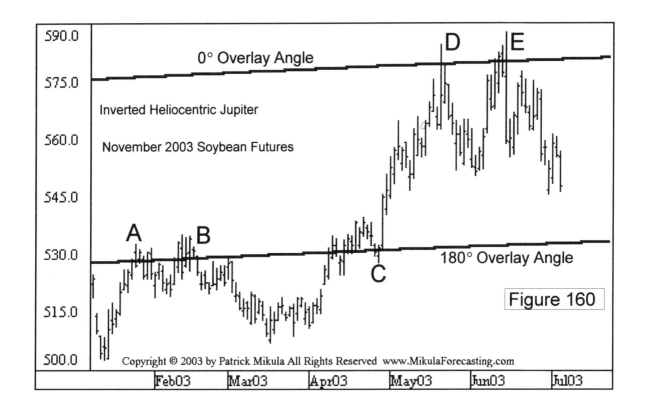

Chapter 15 Review

Objective:
Use Square of Nine planetary angles to locate pivot price levels.

Step 1:
Select a planet to use and mark it's longitude on the outer ring on the Square of Nine.

Step 2:
Align the overlay's 0° angle on the planet's longitude.

Step 3:
Identify the prices which fall on the overlay's angles and are also in the chart price range. The normal overlay angles to use with this method are the 0° angle, the +90° angle, 180° angle and the -90° angle. Using more overlay angles than this, such as the 45° angles, usually creates planetary lines on the chart which are too close together to be of any value.

Step 4:
Drawn the prices found in Step 3 on the chart to create the planetary angles. Watch for pivots to form around these planetary angles.

CHAPTER 16: Mikula's Square of Nine High-Low Forecast Indicator

This chapter shows how to use the mathematics of the Square of Nine to forecast the next bar's high - low range

In the introduction of this book, there is a section entitled "Formula for Moving Around The Square of Nine." Another application of that formula is to calculate technical indicators for forecasting and trading. In this chapter that formula will be used to calculate a forecast for the next bar's high and low. This indicator can be calculated by any program which allows formulas to be written such as a spreadsheet.

Required User Inputs

There are three user inputs for this indicator which are listed below. The *Price Multiplier* input is used for low priced items. If a stock price's whole number has less than three digits, the decimal point is moved to the right by setting this value to 10 or 100. For example if a stock price is 21, this input would be set to 10 so the price used would be 210. If the price is very low such as 1.02, the *Price Multiplier* is set to 100 so the price used would be 102. Using a price which has at least 3 digits in the whole number often works better than the low prices.

The input *High Forecast in Degrees*, is the number of degrees that are moved on the Square of Nine to calculate the forecast for the next bar's high price.

The input *Low Forecast in Degrees*, is the number of degrees moved on the Square of Nine to calculate the forecast for the next bar's low price.

User Inputs	--------
Price Multiplier	1
High Forecast in Degrees	+45 Deg
Low Forecast in Degrees	-45 Deg

Formula and Calculation Procedure

Step 1: Convert the input *High Forecast in Degrees* to a square root value. This is done by dividing the input by 360°, then multiplying by 2. The resulting number is the "High Offset Value". (45° / 360°) * 2 = 0.25

Step 2: Convert the input *Low Forecast in Degrees* to a square root value. This is done by dividing the input by 360°, then multiplying by 2. The resulting number is the "Low Offset Value". (-45° / 360°) * 2 = -0.25

Step 3: If the input *Price Multiplier* is set to 10 or 100, then multiply it by the current closing price. This moves the decimal place to the right to create a higher price.

Step 4: Calculate the square root of the current bar's closing price.
Square root √, 1191.70 = 34.521

Step 5: Add the High Offset Value (Step 1) to the square root of the price (Step 4).
0.25 (Step 1) + 34.521 (Step 4) = 34.771

Step 6: Add Low Offset Value (Step 2) to the square root of the price (Step 4).
-0.25 (Step 2) + 34.521 (Step 4) = 34.271

Step 7: Calculate the 2nd exponent of Step 5. This is the next bar forecast high price.
34.771^2 or (34.771 * 34.771) = 1209.023

Step 8: Calculate the 2nd exponent of Step 6. This is the next bar forecast low price.
34.271^2 or (34.271 * 34.271) = 1174.502

Sample Calculation For Mikula's Square of Nine
High-Low Forecast Indicator

Date	Close	Step 4	Step 5	Step 6	Step 7 Forecast High	Step 8 Forecast Low
2003/06/02	1185.13	34.426	34.676	34.176	------------	------------
2003/06/03	1198.57	34.620	34.870	34.370	1202.405	1167.980
2003/06/04	1224.76	34.997	35.247	34.747	1215.943	1181.322
2003/06/05	1231.72	35.096	35.346	34.846	1242.321	1207.324
2003/06/06	1213.11	34.830	35.080	34.580	1249.330	1214.235
2003/06/09	1195.55	34.577	34.827	34.327	1230.587	1195.758
2003/06/10	1212.99	34.828	35.078	34.578	1212.901	1178.324
2003/06/11	1228.24	35.046	35.296	34.796	1230.467	1195.638
2003/06/12	1229.32	35.062	35.312	34.812	1245.826	1210.779
2003/06/13	1203.91	34.697	34.947	34.447	1246.913	1211.852
2003/06/16	1241.58	35.236	35.486	34.986	1221.321	1186.624
2003/06/17	1239.63	35.208	35.458	34.958	1259.261	1224.024
2003/06/18	1247.90	35.326	35.576	35.076	1257.297	1222.088
2003/06/19	1225.89	35.013	35.263	34.763	1265.625	1230.300
2003/06/20	1223.06	34.972	35.222	34.722	1243.459	1208.446
2003/06/23	1200.17	34.643	34.893	34.393	1240.609	1205.636
2003/06/24	1191.70	34.521	34.771	34.271	1217.554	1182.911
2003/06/25	------------	------------	------------	------------	1209.023	1174.502

CHAPTER 16: Mikula's Square of Nine High-Low Forecast Indicator

This chapter shows how to use the mathematics of the Square of Nine to forecast the next bar's high - low range

In the introduction of this book, there is a section entitled "Formula for Moving Around The Square of Nine." Another application of that formula is to calculate technical indicators for forecasting and trading. In this chapter that formula will be used to calculate a forecast for the next bar's high and low. This indicator can be calculated by any program which allows formulas to be written such as a spreadsheet.

Required User Inputs

There are three user inputs for this indicator which are listed below. The *Price Multiplier* input is used for low priced items. If a stock price's whole number has less than three digits, the decimal point is moved to the right by setting this value to 10 or 100. For example if a stock price is 21, this input would be set to 10 so the price used would be 210. If the price is very low such as 1.02, the *Price Multiplier* is set to 100 so the price used would be 102. Using a price which has at least 3 digits in the whole number often works better than the low prices.

The input *High Forecast in Degrees*, is the number of degrees that are moved on the Square of Nine to calculate the forecast for the next bar's high price.

The input *Low Forecast in Degrees*, is the number of degrees moved on the Square of Nine to calculate the forecast for the next bar's low price.

User Inputs	--------
Price Multiplier	1
High Forecast in Degrees	+45 Deg
Low Forecast in Degrees	-45 Deg

Formula and Calculation Procedure

Step 1: Convert the input *High Forecast in Degrees* to a square root value. This is done by dividing the input by 360°, then multiplying by 2. The resulting number is the "High Offset Value". (45° / 360°) * 2 = 0.25

Step 2: Convert the input *Low Forecast in Degrees* to a square root value. This is done by dividing the input by 360°, then multiplying by 2. The resulting number is the "Low Offset Value". (-45° / 360°) * 2 = -0.25

Step 3: If the input *Price Multiplier* is set to 10 or 100, then multiply it by the current closing price. This moves the decimal place to the right to create a higher price.

Step 4: Calculate the square root of the current bar's closing price.
Square root √, 1191.70 = 34.521

Step 5: Add the High Offset Value (Step 1) to the square root of the price (Step 4).
0.25 (Step 1) + 34.521 (Step 4) = 34.771

Step 6: Add Low Offset Value (Step 2) to the square root of the price (Step 4).
-0.25 (Step 2) + 34.521 (Step 4) = 34.271

Step 7: Calculate the 2nd exponent of Step 5. This is the next bar forecast high price.
34.771^2 or (34.771 * 34.771) = 1209.023

Step 8: Calculate the 2nd exponent of Step 6. This is the next bar forecast low price.
34.271^2 or (34.271 * 34.271) = 1174.502

Sample Calculation For Mikula's Square of Nine
High-Low Forecast Indicator

Date	Close	Step 4	Step 5	Step 6	Step 7 Forecast High	Step 8 Forecast Low
2003/06/02	1185.13	34.426	34.676	34.176	------------	------------
2003/06/03	1198.57	34.620	34.870	34.370	1202.405	1167.980
2003/06/04	1224.76	34.997	35.247	34.747	1215.943	1181.322
2003/06/05	1231.72	35.096	35.346	34.846	1242.321	1207.324
2003/06/06	1213.11	34.830	35.080	34.580	1249.330	1214.235
2003/06/09	1195.55	34.577	34.827	34.327	1230.587	1195.758
2003/06/10	1212.99	34.828	35.078	34.578	1212.901	1178.324
2003/06/11	1228.24	35.046	35.296	34.796	1230.467	1195.638
2003/06/12	1229.32	35.062	35.312	34.812	1245.826	1210.779
2003/06/13	1203.91	34.697	34.947	34.447	1246.913	1211.852
2003/06/16	1241.58	35.236	35.486	34.986	1221.321	1186.624
2003/06/17	1239.63	35.208	35.458	34.958	1259.261	1224.024
2003/06/18	1247.90	35.326	35.576	35.076	1257.297	1222.088
2003/06/19	1225.89	35.013	35.263	34.763	1265.625	1230.300
2003/06/20	1223.06	34.972	35.222	34.722	1243.459	1208.446
2003/06/23	1200.17	34.643	34.893	34.393	1240.609	1205.636
2003/06/24	1191.70	34.521	34.771	34.271	1217.554	1182.911
2003/06/25	------------	------------	------------	------------	1209.023	1174.502

Figure 161 is a graphic example of how this indicator forecasts the high and low. Let's assume the input *High Forecast in Degrees* is +45° and the input *Low Forecast in Degrees* is -45°. If the closing price is 268, a move on the face of the Square of Nine of +45° yields a high forecast of 276. A move of -45° on the face of the Square of Nine yields a low forecast of 260.

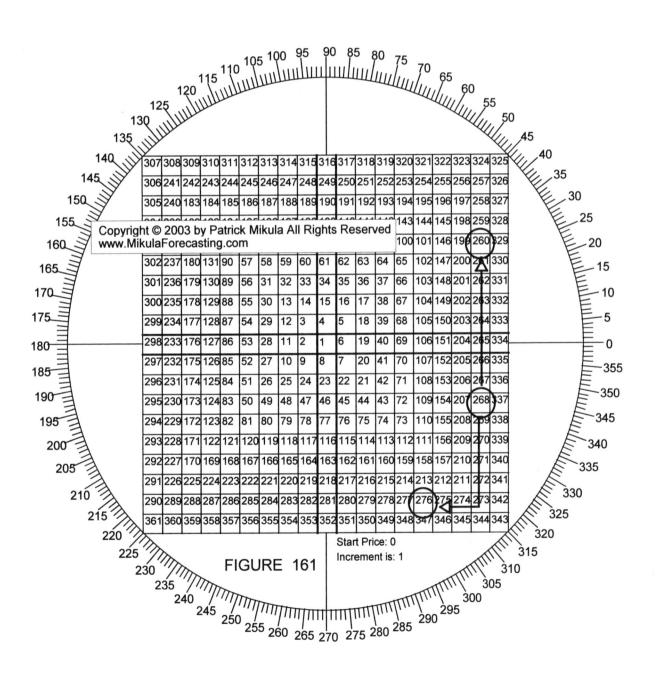

FIGURE 161

Example 1 of Mikula's Square of Nine High-Low Forecast Indicator: Daily NASDAQ Index

Figure 162 shows the NASDAQ index with the forecast high and low on the chart. In the majority of cases, a bar's high - low range falls between the forecast high - low range. The forecast high - low range provides an expectation of where the next bar should form under normal circumstances.

If a bar's high price moves above the forecast high price, it is a show of market strength. If a bar's closing price is above the forecast high, it is a very strong indication. When this occurs, watch the market for more upward movement.

If a bar's low price moves below the forecast low price, it is a show of market weakness. If a bar's closing price is below the low forecast, it is a very weak showing. This weakness in the market is often followed by a downswing.

When these forecast high and low values are calculated on a daily chart, they can be used as the expected price range by intraday traders. An intraday trader can use these values as the support and resistance levels on the intraday chart.

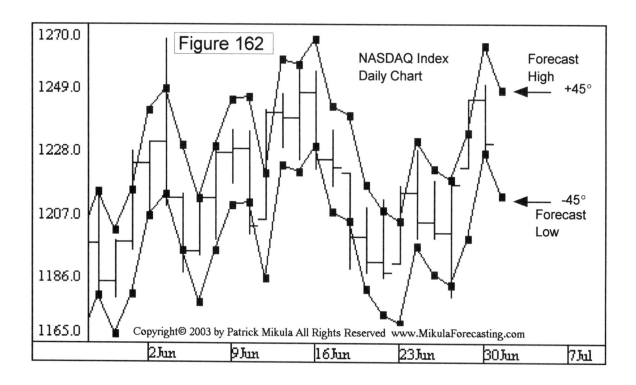

Example 2 of Mikula's Square of Nine High-Low Forecast Indicator: Daily Soybeans

Figure 163 shows the November 2003 Soybean market. The High - Low Forecast Indicator, is applied with the input *High Forecast in Degrees* set to +30° and the input *Low Forecast in Degrees* set to -30°. This indicator provides the trader with a good expectation as to the location of the next bar's high low range. The majority of the price bars are inside the forecast high low range. When a price bar closes below the low forecast, it shows weakness. When a price bar closes above the high forecast, it shows market strength.

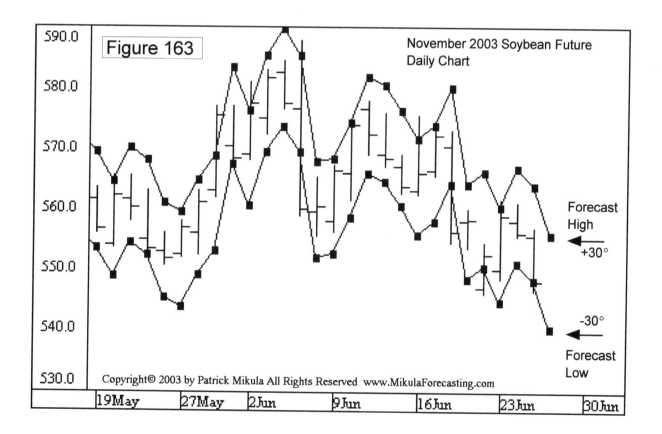

Chapter 16 Review

Objective:
Forecast the high low range for the next price bar.

Rule 1.) The majority of price bars form between the forecast high and low.

Rule 2.) When a bar's high price moves above the high forecast, there is an indication of strength.

Rule 3.) When a bar's low price moves below the low forecast, there is an indication of weakness.

Rule 4.) When a bar closes above the high forecast, there is an indication of an upward breakout and an upswing may follow.

Rule 5.) When a bar closes below the low forecast, there is an indication of a downward breakout and a downswing may follow.

CHAPTER 17: Mikula's Square of Nine Overextended Indicator

This chapter shows how to use the mathematics of the Square of Nine to determine when a market is overextended

This chapter again uses the mathematics which is explained in the introductory section, "Formula for Moving Around The Square of Nine" on page 15. The formula is used to calculate the distance traveled around the face of the Square of Nine that a market has moved above or below a moving average. This allows a trader to determine when the market has moved 45°, 90° or 180° above or below the moving average. Such a movement indicates the market is overextended. When the market is overextended a reversal can be expected.

Required User Inputs

This indicator has five inputs which must be set by the user. The input named *Price Multiplier* is set at either 10 or 100 to move the decimal point of low priced stocks. The inputs named *Upper Line 2 in Degrees* and *Upper Line 1 in Degrees* are the upper boundaries which are used to determine how far above the moving average the price moves. The inputs named *Lower Line 1 in Degrees* and *Lower Line 2 in Degrees* are the lower boundaries used to determine how far below the moving average the price moves. The input named *Moving Average Size* is the sample size for the moving average.

User Inputs	--------
Price Multiplier	10
Upper Line 2 in Degrees	+90 Deg
Upper Line 1 in Degrees	+45 Deg
Lower Line 1 in Degrees	-45 Deg
Lower Line 2 in Degrees	-90 Deg
Moving Average Size	9

Formula and Calculation Procedure

Step 1: Use the input *Moving Average Size* to calculate a simple moving average of the closing price.

Step 2: Multiply the input *Price Multiplier* and the closing price. This step moves the decimal point in the stock's price. For example, if the stock price is below 100, the price multiplier should be 10.

Step 3: Multiply the *Price Multiplier* and the moving average calculated in step 1. This step will move the decimal point in the moving average.

Step 4: Calculate the square root √ of the value from Step 2.

Step 5: Calculate the square root √ of the value from Step 3.

Step 6: Subtract the value derived in Step 4 from the value found in Step 5. This is the difference between the closing price and the moving average calculated as the difference between their respective square roots.

Step 7: Multiply the value from Step 6 by 360 and divide the result by 2. This converts the square root value back to degrees. This value is the degrees on the face of the Square of Nine between the closing price and the moving average.

Step 8: Calculate a 2 period moving average of the value found in step 7. This is done to smooth the result.

Sample Calculation For Mikula's Square of Nine
Overextended Indicator

Date	Close	Step 1	Step 2	Step 3	Step 4	Step 5
2003/06/02	11.07	------------	------------	------------	------------	------------
2003/06/03	10.69	------------	------------	------------	------------	------------
2003/06/04	10.56	------------	------------	------------	------------	------------
2003/06/05	10.60	------------	------------	------------	------------	------------
2003/06/06	10.71	------------	------------	------------	------------	------------
2003/06/09	10.52	------------	------------	------------	------------	------------
2003/06/10	11.00	------------	------------	------------	------------	------------
2003/06/11	11.33	------------	------------	------------	------------	------------
2003/06/12	11.27	10.861	112.700	108.611	10.616	10.422
2003/06/13	10.97	10.850	109.700	108.500	10.474	10.416
2003/06/16	11.23	10.910	112.300	109.100	10.597	10.445
2003/06/17	11.68	11.034	116.800	110.344	10.807	10.504
2003/06/18	11.52	11.137	115.200	111.367	10.733	10.553
2003/06/19	11.28	11.200	112.800	112.000	10.621	10.583
2003/06/20	11.52	11.311	115.200	113.111	10.733	10.635
2003/06/23	11.30	11.344	113.000	113.444	10.630	10.651
2003/06/24	11.35	11.347	113.500	113.467	10.654	10.652
2003/06/25	11.21	11.340	112.100	113.400	10.588	10.649

Date	Step 6	Step 7	Step 8
2003/06/02	------------	------------	------------
2003/06/03	------------	------------	------------
2003/06/04	------------	------------	------------
2003/06/05	------------	------------	------------
2003/06/06	------------	------------	------------
2003/06/09	------------	------------	------------
2003/06/10	------------	------------	------------
2003/06/11	------------	------------	------------
2003/06/12	0.19	34.98	------------
2003/06/13	0.06	10.34	22.66
2003/06/16	0.15	27.37	18.86
2003/06/17	0.30	54.52	40.95
2003/06/18	0.18	32.42	43.47
2003/06/19	0.04	6.79	19.60
2003/06/20	0.10	17.60	12.19
2003/06/23	-0.02	-3.76	6.92
2003/06/24	0.00	0.28	-1.74
2003/06/25	-0.06	-11.02	-5.37

Example 1 of Mikula's Square of Nine Overextended Indicator:
Daily Corn

Figure 164 shows this indicator applied to the December 2003 Corn contract. The two upper boundaries are set at +45° and +90°. The two lower boundaries are set at -45° and -90°. The moving average sample size is set to 15. The flat horizontal line drawn through the middle of the subgraph represents the position of the moving average. The oscillator represents how many degrees the current price is above or below the 15 bar moving average on the face of the Square of Nine.

When the oscillator moves above the first upper boundary at point A, it is 45° above the moving average. This signals that the market is becoming overextended to the upside and a market pull back can be expected. At point B, the market moves below the first lower boundary. This indicates the price is -45° below the moving average on the face of the Square of Nine. This means the market is overextended to the downside and a market rally should be expected over the next series of bars.

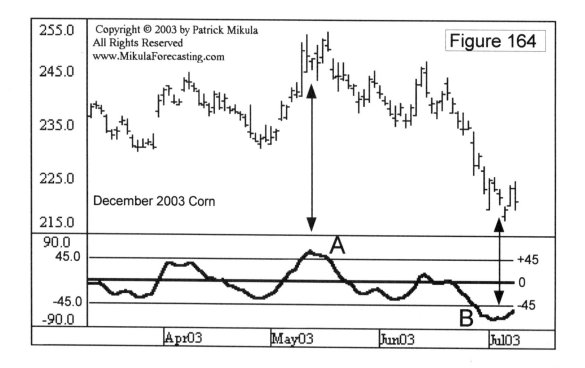

Example 2 of Mikula's Square of Nine Overextended Indicator:
Daily Johnson & Johnson, JNJ

Figure 165 shows a daily chart for Johnson and Johnson. The user inputs are set as follows. The price of this stock is below 100 so the input Price Multiplier is set to 10. The moving average sample size is set to 15. The upper boundaries are set to +90° and +180° and the lower boundaries are set to -180° and -90°. The flat horizontal line in the center of the subgraph illustrates the position of the moving average on the Square of Nine.

At point A, the oscillator moves above the first upper boundary. This indicates the price is now 90° above the moving average on the face of the Square of Nine and the market is becoming overextended. At point B, the oscillator falls to the first lower boundary. This indicates the price is now -90° below the moving average on the Square of Nine and this means the market is becoming overextended to the downside. For a second time, at point C, the price is -90° below the moving average on the Square of Nine. When the price becomes overextended, a swing reversal can be expected.

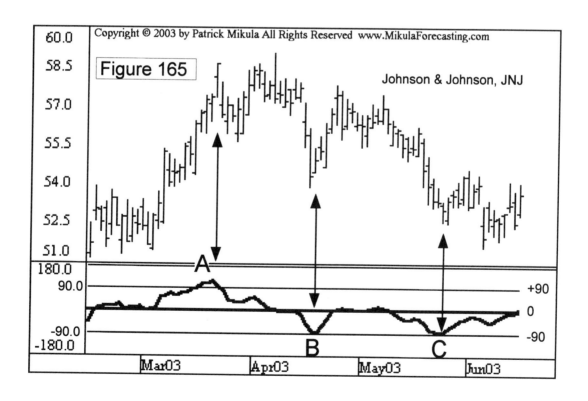

Example 3 of Mikula's Square of Nine Overextended Indicator: Daily Baker Hughs Inc. BHI

Figure 166 shows this indicator applied to Baker Hughes, BHI, which is an oil exploration and services firm. The indicator inputs are set as follows. The moving average sample size set to 15. The price of this stock is below 100 so the Price Multiplier input is set to 10. The upper boundaries are set to +90° and +180°. The lower boundaries are set to -90° and -180°.

The oscillator falls to the first lower boundary at point A. This means the price is -90° below the moving average on the Square of Nine. This is a sign that the market may have a rally soon. The same situation occurs at point B and again the oscillator indicates the market may form a bottom pivot.

At both points C and D, the oscillator moves up to the first upper boundary. This means the oscillator is +90° above the moving average on the Square of Nine. At points C and D, watch for the market to make a pivot top because the indicator shows the market is overextended.

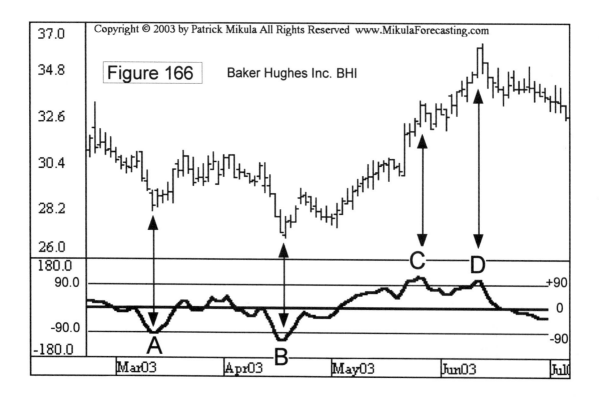

Chapter 17 Review

Objective:
Determine if a market is overextended too far upward or downward.

Rule 1.) When the oscillator moves +45°, +90° or +180° above the moving average, there is an indication that the market is overextended upward. When this occurs, watch for a pivot reversal.

Rule 2.) When the oscillator moves -45°, -90° or -180° below the moving average, there is an indication the market is overextended too far downward. Watch for a pivot reversal.

APPENDIX 1: Index of Commodity Values

Contract	Symbol	Exchange	Contract Size	Trading Hours in CT	Minimum Tick
Grains					
Soymeal	SM	CBOT	100 ton	9:30 am - 1:15 pm	10 pts = $10
Bean Oil	BO	CBOT	60,000 lbs	9:30 am - 1:15 pm	1 pt = $6
Corn	C	CBOT	5,000 bu	9:30 am - 1:15 pm	1/4 ct = $12.50
Oats	O	CBOT	5,000 bu	9:30 am - 1:15 pm	1/4 ct = $12.50
Soybeans	S	CBOT	5,000 bu	9:30 am - 1:15 pm	1/4 ct = $12.50
Wheat (CBOT)	W	CBOT	5,000 bu	9:30 am - 1:15 pm	1/4 ct = $12.50
Metals					
Gold	GC	COMEX	100 Troy oz	7:20 am - 12:30 pm	10 cts = $10
Copper	HG	COMEX	25,000 lbs	7:10 am - 12:00 pm	5 pts = $12.50
Palladium	PA	COMEX	100 Troy oz	7:30 am - 12:00 pm	5 pts = $5
Platinum	PL	COMEX	50 Troy oz	7:20 am - 12:05 pm	10 cts = $5
Silver	SI	COMEX	5,000 Troy oz	7:25 am - 12:25 pm	1/2 ct = $25
Currencies					
Australian Dollar	AD	CME	100,000 AD	7:20 am - 2:00 pm	1 pt = $10
British Pound	BP	CME	62,500 BP	7:20 am - 2:00 pm	2 pts = $12.50
Canadian Dollar	CD	CME	100,000 CD	7:20 am - 2:00 pm	1 pt = $10
US Dollar Index	DX	NYBOT	1,000 x index	7:20 am - 2:00 pm	1 pt = $10
Euro Currency	EC	CME	125,000 euro	7:20 am - 2:00 pm	1 pt = $12.50
Japanese Yen	JY	CME	12.5 M yen	7:20 am - 2:00 pm	1 pt = $12.50
Swiss Franc	SF	CME	125,000 SF	7:20 am - 2:00 pm	1 pt = $12.50
Financials					
Dow Jones	DJ	CBOT	$10 x DJIA	7:20 am - 3:15 pm	1 pt = $10
Eurodollar	ED	CME	1000000	7:20 am - 2:00 pm	1/2 pt = $12.50
Nasdaq 100	ND	CME	$100 x index	8:30 am - 3:15 pm	5 pts = $5
S&P 500	SP	CME	$250 x index	8:30 am - 3:15 pm	10 pts = $25
30-Year Bond	US	CBOT	100000	7:20 am - 2:00 pm	1 pt = $31.25

Contract	Symbol	Exchange	Contract Size	Trading Hours in CT	Minimum Tick
Energies	--------------	--------------	--------------	--------------	--------------
Crude Oil	CL	NYMEX	1,000 barrels	9:00 am - 1:30 pm	1 ct = $10
Heating Oil	HO	NYMEX	42,000 gallons	9:05 am - 1:30 pm	1 pt = $4.20
Natural Gas	NG	NYMEX	10,000 MMBTU	9:00 am - 1:30 pm	1 pt = $10
Unleaded Gas	HU	NYMEX	42,000 gallons	9:05 am - 1:30 pm	1 pt = $4.20
Softs	--------------	--------------	--------------	--------------	--------------
Cocoa	CO	CSCE	10 tonnes	7:00 am - 10:50 am	1 pt = $10
Coffee	KC	CSCE	37,500 lbs	8:00 am - 10:45 am	5 pts = $18.75
Cotton	CT	Cotton Exc	50,000 lbs	11:15 am - 2:00 pm	1 pt = $5
FCOJ	OJ	Cotton Exc	15,000 lbs	11:30 am - 1:45 pm	5 pts = $7.50
Sugar	SB	CSCE	112,000 lbs	8:00 am - 11:00 am	1 pt = $11.20
Meats	--------------	--------------	--------------	--------------	--------------
Feeder Cattle	FC	CME	50,000 lbs	9:05 am - 1:00 pm	2.5 pts = $12.50
Lean Hogs	LH	CME	40,000 lbs	9:10 am - 1:00 pm	2.5 pts = $10
Live Cattle	LC	CME	40,000 lbs	9:05 am - 1:00 pm	2.5 pts = $10
Pork Bellies	PB	CME	40,000 lbs	9:10 am - 1:00 pm	2.5 pts = $10

NOTES

NOTES

NOTES

NOTES

NOTES